The Love Principles

Kathleen,
may these principles
continue to expand
your consciousness.
with love,
Arleen
/osw

9/01

Other Books by Arleen Lorrance

The Love Project

Channeling Love Energy
(with Diane K. Pike)

Buddha from Brooklyn

Musings for Meditation

Why Me? How to Heal
What's Hurting You

The Love Project Way
(with Diane K. Pike)

Born of Love

India through Eyes of Love

Images

THE
LOVE
PRINCIPLES

by

Arleen Lorrance

Teleos Imprint ~ *Scottsdale, AZ*

Teleos Imprint
Wisdom Books
Published by LP Publications
7119 E. Shea Blvd.
Suite 109 PMB 418
Scottsdale, AZ 85254-6107

The Teleos Institute World Wide Web site address is
http://www.consciousnesswork.com

Library of Congress Cataloguing-in-Publication Data

Lorrance, Arleen, 1939-
   The love principles / by Arleen Lorrance.
        p. cm.
   ISBN 0-916192-45-8 (alk. paper)
1. Love--Psychic aspects. I. Title.
   BF1045.L7 L67 2001
   131-dc21

                                    2001002822
                                        CIP

Printed in the United States of America

Cover photo by Arleen Lorrance

Teleos Imprint
Cascade of Angels

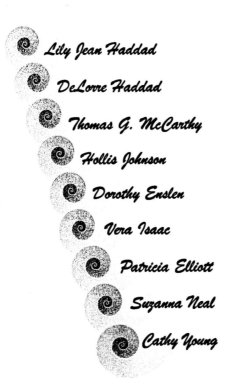

Lily Jean Haddad

DeLorre Haddad

Thomas G. McCarthy

Hollis Johnson

Dorothy Enslen

Vera Isaac

Patricia Elliott

Suzanna Neal

Cathy Young

Would you like to be included in our cascade of angels?
Call 480-471-3082 or e-mail ljh4848@aol.com.

ACKNOWLEDGMENTS

Thousands of people have worked with **The Love Principles** over the last three decades and changed not only their own lives, but also the world around them. But I think especially of the *Seekers*, the first to embrace the principles, a group of students at Thomas Jefferson High School in Brooklyn, New York, who devoted themselves to unconditional love and to making their school a place of harmony. I am grateful that individuals made and make the choice to learn to love.

Special recognition to **Lily Jean Haddad**, a graduate of The Theatre of Life, a teacher of Life as a Waking Dream, a Minister in The Order of Teleos, a bright ray of light in my life, and, a tireless supporter of the work of Teleos Institute. Through her efforts, Teleos Imprint became a reality and published this book.

Great thanks to the **Cascade of Angels** listed in the front of this book who made major contributions to Teleos Institute to launch Teleos Imprint and allow us to offer our knowledge of the Ancient Wisdom in a variety of forms.

I appreciate those who made specific financial contributions toward the publishing of this particular volume. And I am especially indebted to all those who, over the last 30 years, have embraced and disseminated **The Love Principles.** Through their promotion of workshops in their communities, by handing out little yellow cards on which **The Love Principles** are printed, and through their own embodiment of the **Principles,** they have opened the way for love to transform lives.

Above all, I am grateful to my partner, Mariamne Paulus, a.k.a. Diane Kennedy Pike, for being a perfect spiritual companion since 1972. There is little that is more gratifying or powerful than having by your side someone who is equally devoted to the Wisdom – to living it, to expressing it. I am blessed.

— *Arleen Lorrance*
Scottsdale, Arizona

For

Millie Boucher
and
Carl Downing

Two who embraced and lived
The Love Principles,
Two who shared the process
of living and dying,
Two who taught each other about
unconditional love.

THE LOVE PRINCIPLES

received in 1970
by Arleen Lorrance

- ◆ Have no expectations,
  but rather
  abundant expectancy.

- ◆ Create your own reality
  consciously.

- ◆ Receive all people
  as beautiful
  exactly as they are.

- ◆ Be the change you want
  to see happen instead of
  trying to change anyone else.

- ◆ Provide others with
  opportunities to give.

- ◆ Problems are opportunities.

TABLE OF CONTENTS

AUTHOR'S NOTE

For the past 30 years, I have been learning about love. During that time, I have experienced and witnessed love's pitfalls and power. I have known its pains and exaltations. Of all things on earth, love is the simplest. Yet, paradoxically, the misuse of love and the misunderstanding of love cause more suffering than satisfaction in most individuals. I count myself among those who have agonized. My struggle, however, has been one of growth. Through six incisive keys known as **The Love Principles**, I have found *the power of conscious loving*.

These principles have enabled me to have what I call "creative jurisdiction" over my life, my choices, my feelings, my thoughts, and my responses. I have liberated myself from debilitating unhappiness so that I am no longer the victim of love's throes. Instead, love's true nature has remarkably enhanced me. I have learned how to remain open in all circumstances and relationships. In the past, I suffered often. Now I transform pain into life-affirming action.

The principles have been popularized over the last twenty-five years and they have found their way into common usage. When most people refer to them, they use them singly. But the real power of the principles comes when they are used all together in a single circumstance. For example, if I acknowledge that a physical dis-ease is an opportunity, I am well on my way to setting healing energy in motion. However, if I have specific expectations, rather than expectancy, about *how* the healing will occur, I may miss my opportunity when it presents itself in an unanticipated guise.

Using all the principles in concert is what completely and positively altered my life.

I received **The Love Principles** at the end of October 1970. I use the word "received" rather than "channeled" because "channeled" implies that the principles came from a magical source outside of self. Many who channel do not remember what they said because it was said "through them," not by them. This may seem, at first, to add greater validity to what they are offering.

My experience was different. I "received" the principles because I was ready to hear this wisdom that is available to anyone who is ready. I was prepared to live it, to be a model of it, and to teach it. Therefore, when the principles were given, I wrote them down and was fully conscious that they were a gift to me as well as to others.

In 1968 I experienced the opening of my heart center. On the physical level, it took the form of heart disease, caused by a virus. I dealt with issues of survival and healing for six-months. During that time, I began to discover that I was filled with gratitude and appreciation, that I loved more universally, and, that I was in a constant state of love. In 1969, I began spiritual studies that showed me that my heart episode was an awakening.

After studying seriously for about a year, I began to attend what I experienced as classes in my sleep. The phenomenon was very different from dreaming. My teachers were not visible to the eye. The communications were in energy rather than words. Each night it was as if I was taken to classrooms deeper in the interior of the "school." I began to realize that as I learned and assimilated what I was being taught, I was given more advanced material.

As I woke in the morning, I experienced a descent through levels of consciousness until I awoke "as myself in my bed." I knew that something profound had happened in the sleep-learning session but I couldn't put any of it into words. I learned the reason for this soon after the instruction stopped. It was that I would not be able to remember until and unless I was prepared to become what I had been taught.

The test of this came during a serious fight in the auditorium of the tough ghetto high school where I was teaching at the time. Two boys were ready to kill each other and over a hundred classmates were egging them on to tragedy. Without hesitating, I ran into the center of the turmoil and placed myself between the two combatants. I did not think of my safety. I knew that this was a critical moment for me, and that I was being called upon to be a force of love in the midst of what promised to be a blood bath.

I reached to the two from the power of heart center love and touched each of them as I separated them. Looking both of them in the eyes, I called them to a higher level of functioning than they had chosen. Despite the screams of their opposing entourages, the boys relinquished their fury, then turned and left the scene of the altercation.

I stood right where I had planted myself, shaking from head to toe, unable to move. I felt struck by the power of love, and lighted in the midst of a dark storm of potential violence. Everyone dispersed. As I exhaled, I knew that I had passed a test, that I had embodied a commitment. I felt transformed, as if by a mystical experience.

A few minutes later, I rejoined my class in our classroom and we wept together over the horrendous conditions that dominated our learning environment. We pledged to each other that somehow we would find a way to bring about change.

At the bell, I retreated to my office, weary from the total event. Then, in the stillness, there came a ray of light. In the illumination, **The Love Principles** were given. I did not hear them spoken as words. I felt them as if they were fine music played on an unseen instrument. As I wrote them down, I immediately realized that these principles represented what I had learned in my sleep. Because I had risked my life and taken a stand in love, I could now "remember" the profound learning.

I acted upon the principles immediately by starting **The Love Project*** at the high school. **The Love Principles** completely changed the school environment for the better, and they completely changed the way I lived my life. The mundane had been transmuted into a state akin to Grace. I felt blessed and my objective became to bless others with the wonder of what I had come to know.

The Love Principles can liberate you from the inconstancy of love as a feeling, and from the limited nature of love as an expression. I offer the principles to

---

*The full story is written in *The Love Project*, by Arleen Lorrance, 1972.

you, the reader, because I have come to know compassion, bliss, creativity, hope, and unshakable strength by living them.

The Love Principles can open our hearts to tender and unconditional regard for each other. When used together, the six principles can positively alter the nature of human relationship.

The Love Principles have facilitated profound changes in hundreds of people who have worked and studied personally with me over the last three decades. To this day, at workshops and presentations across the continent, individuals come up to show me the "little yellow card" they carry in their wallets. It contains the six principles that have served them steadfastly over the years. In many cases, the little yellow card is battered from excessive use but the carrier rejects replacing the "old friend" with a new one.

Many thousands of people have benefited from embodying the principles and have changed their lives for the better. I am offering what I have come to know so that countless others might experience the true power of love.

WHAT IS LOVE?

When I was growing up, love was huckleberry pie. My father brought it home every Saturday night when he finished his second job as a shoe salesman. He brought thick, blue-black huckleberry pie that stained my teeth and had me closing my eyes as I savored it before swallowing. That was love.

No one in my family was very affectionate. I craved hugging, touching, embracing. I settled for pies, 7-layer cakes, napoleons and chocolate eclairs.

My father left before dawn for his primary job as a cutter in the garment district of New York City. In the evenings, he sold shoes. He made a living for his family standing on his feet for 12 hours a day and that was his expression of love. After six days of work a week, 50 weeks a year, he had very little energy left for affectionate expressions.

My mother showed her love through total devotion to her children. She watched over everything we did and smothered us with worry. She loved us through her control, domination, and rule of the family.

While I was cared for in all the basic ways and encouraged to fulfill my potential, I never felt loved by anyone in my family; at least, not in ways that would fit my definition. It was not that we weren't expressive people. Our emotions exploded in volume and intensity.

But when it came to tenderness and kindness, bitter lemon was more prevalent than sweet nectar.

I spent most of my early life searching for love's softness. Along the way of my search, I met others who were similarly deprived. We appeared whole and well adjusted, but our inner selves were wounded. We were burdened by unmet needs that held us back even as we pushed forward with great ambition and desire.

During my adult years, I found what I had been seeking. I had many opportunities to be loved and to love. Yet surprisingly, even as my various images about love were fulfilled, the satisfaction that came as a result was fleeting. I was gratified on the personality level, but a hunger continued in my spirit. My needs were being met and I was meeting the needs of others. However, as if my life were a stretch of farmland, a new crop of needs broke ground with regularity and it seemed I required continuous tending.

It was then that I began to realize that love is more than a need. That realization enabled me to turn a corner. Instead of longing for specific expressions or for the fulfillment of particular desires, I longed for meaning, for inner peace. The six **Love Principles** helped me achieve that goal.

Where before there was emptiness, now everything is an exciting discovery. I constantly uncover the profound even in the mundane. Each day is an adventure in growing and changing.

It is in life meaning, life purpose, and wholeness that the *true* love becomes manifest.

We are living in a time of such rapid change that we can barely keep up. In our shrinking world, the electronics revolution has impersonalized our interactions. While we communicate with great speed and efficiency, we have fewer meaningful connections with one an-other. This deficiency has been experienced as a loss of meaning in our lives.

We yearn to make a difference in the world, to matter, to leave an imprint of value. We desire to love, yet we need to know *how* to love. Uncertainty sur-rounds us and we are searching for a sense of security. Huckleberry pie can't satiate our quest, nor can being held or hugged. Nothing short of personal transforma-tion will meet the spiritual burning within our souls.

It seems the quest for meaning is permeating the very air we breathe. Our profound desire for deeper un-derstanding and for clarity is unmistakable. In this new Aquarian Age, we question our former beliefs. We resist following the flock and exercising blind faith. Instead, we seek direct *knowing* through personal experience. We know it is time for us to take full responsibility for our thoughts, actions, and feelings.

The **Love Principles** served me in my awakening and renewal. They enabled me to function with mean-ing and purpose. I have watched them do the same for thousands of others. The principles are not a quick fix. They require commitment. When *all* the principles are lived they provide a steady, reliable transformational process over a long period of time. They expedite the touching of new heights as a human being. Even after three decades of practicing them, I am still in the pro-cess of being transformed.

I received the **Love Principles** in October 1970 while I was teaching at a ghetto high school in Brooklyn, New York. The embodiment of these principles changed the school in a nine-month period from a place of vio-lence, negativity, and minimal learning, to a center of caring, joy, and growth-filled education. Since then, with my colleague, Diane Kennedy Pike, I have disseminated the principles across the continent and in many places throughout the world.

Since their inception, the principles have become integrated into general language usage. They were part of a large wave of change that began in the 1960's when there was growing awareness of the need for universal love and of how important it is to take personal responsibility for reality creation.

Throughout the last 30 years I have had ample opportunities to prove to myself that when I activate these principles I am engaged in loving of the highest order. The principles guide me to functioning consciously, hopefully, unconditionally, creatively, and dynamically. They facilitate inner peace and enable the one using them to engage powerfully in any life circumstance.

★ ★ ★

Defining love is not easy. Even the third edition of Webster's *New World Dictionary* offers a potpourri of choices:
1. a deep and tender feeling of affection for or attachment or devotion to a person or persons
2. an expression of one's affection
3. a feeling of brotherhood and good will toward other people
4. strong liking or interest in something.
5. a strong, usually passionate, affection of one person for another, based in part on sexual attraction
6. sexual intercourse
7. God's tender regard for humankind.

Language represents our collective state of consciousness. The words we use, and the meanings they convey, reveal our knowledge and understanding to date. These dictionary definitions tell me that culturally we perceive love primarily as a feeling and only secondarily as an expression.

If love is a feeling, it is fickle, because feelings are sensitivities and sensations that are in a constant state of flux. Hence, we can love someone one minute and hate him the next. We can be in love and out of love in a flash. My experience has shown me that feeling love, or being in love, is very different from *being* love or *embodying* love.

If love is an expression, it can easily be misunderstood or misinterpreted. These days, a smile can be construed as harassment and a touch on the shoulder proclaimed a sexual advance. Others can see what some would call an act of kindness as interference. Another can experience what one person intends as a generous gift as insulting or degrading.

The dictionary definition that comes closest to what love really is, as I have come to know it, is the last one given: God's tender regard for humankind. This tender regard is unconditional. It goes beyond feeling or expression to an unrestricted flow of energy.

It surprises me that the dictionary applies this powerful definition to God and not to human beings. Since the dictionary is representative of our collective state of consciousness, we are the ones who have separated ourselves from the true power of love because we imply that we cannot love as God loves.

We have toyed with the spiritual dimension of love for millennia. We have proclaimed that perfect love casts out all fear. But what is perfect love? Surely the answer remains generally unknown because fear is rampant on our planet. This becomes painfully evident when we realize that the world's leading democracy, the United States of America, has over 200 million firearms in circulation.

Sometimes I think that the human race is more afraid of love than of anything else. I watch people hesitate to say "I love you" to others because they don't know how the other will take that statement or where it might lead. And others are reluctant to act on behalf of someone who is in danger for fear of lawsuits or reprisals.

Love is seen as inappropriate in the workplace because it is not businesslike. Men who would hug each other in the office would be suspect. Women who would love their fellow male workers would be asking for trouble and vice versa.

Love does not seem to belong in the schools because adults making physical contact with children would definitely raise eyebrows. Are they child molesters?

How can we even begin to think about perfect love when we do not know what love is and when we limit it to feeings, or to sex? Collectively, we are like awkward teenagers, breaking out with emotional acne because feelings of warmth and caring stir in us and we haven't a clue about how or if to give them life.

The daily newspapers tell us in repeated stories how easily people hate or kill each other. The fact that there are hardly ever stories about people loving one another is a sad commentary on the human race.

I often allow myself to imagine a world in which everyone is committed to embodying divine love, unconditional love. It would be a world in which everyone would have a tender regard for everyone else. I become as giddy as if I'd had a glass of wine at the very thought. To live in such a world would be like having Holy Communion every day!

There can never be a world like this unless it begins with me, with each of us. Even if no one else is doing it, we must. Even when we are rejected or laughed at, we need to begin. How? By activating the **Love Principles**.

We can harness the power of love by **being the change we want to see happen,** no matter what anyone else is doing or refusing to do. If we see what needs to happen, we can become the change ourselves. First, we need to know, not just believe but know, that we can **consciously create the reality** of unconditional love in ourselves. Once we start that flow of creativity, it increases with every breath we take. We can then mirror the new reality for others. We can reach to everyone with tenderness and kindness and honor their uniqueness by **providing them with the opportunity to give** of themselves. We can be models in times of crises, showing those around us that love can prevail in all circumstances because **problems are opportunities**. We can live in expanded states by **having no expectations** and opening ourselves to boundless possibilities. Above all, we can be walking examples of those who love as God loves by **receiving all people as beautiful exactly as they are**.

This is no easy task. It requires commitment and self-development. It requires choosing to love this way in the most difficult of circumstances. My partner and I lost $60,000 in much needed contracts because the granting foundation and the hiring agency director were embroiled in a dispute. Both sides assured us that they held us in the highest regard and that the issues had nothing to do with us. We knew that this was true. Nonetheless, they did not follow through on their promises and left us in the lurch of non-income for a six-month period. They apologized, but they reneged. It was an enormous opportunity for us!

In most of myself, I functioned consciously and powerfully in the face of this crisis. I breathed often and deeply, reminding myself that this **problem was an opportunity.** I had a good deal of writing I needed to do and several months of time had been freed in which to do it.

I reminded myself that though others say they are going to do something, and even say so with great enthusiasm, it does not necessarily mean it is going to happen. Everything needs to be approached with **no expectations but rather abundant expectancy**. In this case, a part of me crossed the line. I really wanted this work to come to fruition, and when it did not, I was terribly disappointed. I clearly had had expectations.

Worse than having expectations, I did not **consciously create a reality** of open, flowing energy. I was not only distressed. I was resentful. "After all," a nagging, small voice of self whined, "what do they care? They go on collecting their salaries. They really don't give a damn what happens to me." This voice repeatedly caused me to shut down my love energy. It disenabled me from **receiving them as beautiful exactly as they were**. I was blocked in relation to them and therefore could not function powerfully. In part, this meant that I could not see how **to be the change I wanted to see happen.**

Every time I thought I had worked through my resistance, I found that I was still stuck. It was exasperating to me because by then I had been practicing and teaching the **Love Principles** for 25 years. It was easy to say I should know better. What was more correct was that vigilance is required in the practice of conscious loving and any of us can slip at any time.

After much work with the incident, I saw that I could not remove my resistance to those who reneged because I was not dealing with the underlying feeling that was predominant. I felt hurt. I had been let down by people I trusted and it was painful. I did not want to feel the pain, so I took on resistance instead. Until I could acknowledge the hurt, and that it was related to several other times in my life when I suffered the same kind of disappointment, I could not move on. I could not love those involved.

* * *

What is love? *Love is unblocked life energy that is conveyed unconditionally through the heart center.* To know this is to know its power.

"Unblocked" signifies free passage. There is no congestion, no separation. Unblocked life energy unconditionally flowing through the heart center allows for union, for merging, for a sense of knowing that surpasses understanding. Unblocked life energy is perfect love. The **Love Principles** are one way of keeping the life flow open and moving.

Where there is unblocked energy, there is openness to the unknown. There is an unconditional response to life that clears the way for the possibility of all things. In time, when increasing numbers of us embody true love, the dictionaries will reflect the change in our consciousness with a new definition.

Wherever there is blockage, there is conflict, either internal or external.

I remember when a young friend told his father that he was a homosexual. His father suffered such despair and shock that he could not talk to his son. He had **expectations** that his oldest son would marry and have children. He felt the news as a stab to his chest and he was momentarily unable to breathe. This **problem** was not received as an **opportunity** for him. He loved his son but he could not let that love flow to him unconditionally. He could not **receive him as beautiful exactly as he was**.

They both suffered from the severing of their relationship. The father blocked his feelings and suffered in silence. This blocking resulted first in the dysfunctional behavior of isolation and denial. The father simply could not **provide** his son **with an opportunity to give** to him by sharing about his lifestyle.

Then the condition worsened. The blockage moved beyond the father's emotional component of self to his physical body. He developed lung cancer and he traced it back to the moment when he felt the imagined stab strike his chest. He could see that he had helped to **create this reality**, but not **consciously**. He died within a very short time, never having come to terms with his feelings about his son.

Had the father been able to love, to relate to his son with unblocked life energy, with an unconditional flow from his heart center, he might have wept. His tears would have been a gift to his son. He might have expressed his inability to handle difficult situations, or his disappointment, or his fears. He might have asked for help professionally or from family. Had he expressed his love and his pain, he might still be alive today. He had wanted a significant relationship with his son but he was not able to **be the change he wanted to see happen**.

Love is unblocked life energy, expressed through the heart center, unconditionally. Once I began embodying this knowledge, I became increasingly empowered. For example, I was less intimidated by threatening interactions.

One of my first experiences with feeling more empowered came while I was serving as assistant dean of girls in that tough ghetto high school. I disciplined two girls who had engaged in a serious fistfight, and they were instructed to return with their parents the next day. As the combatants left my office in their continuing rage, one of them turned to me and said, with a menacing expression, "My mother and me are gonna break your ass." As she left, I took a deep breath. I might have panicked, but I didn't. I knew immediately that she needed to say that, simply to maintain her stature. I also knew that she hadn't had a chance to expend all of her fight energy because the battle had been interrupted. I sat quietly and held the two girls in my heart center, breathing out love to each of them, **receiving them as beautiful exactly as they were**. I had no idea how they would behave the next day, but I was very clear about how I wanted to conduct myself during the exchange. It was up to me to **be the change I wanted to see happen** during our meeting.

The two girls and their mothers were hostile and angry when they showed up in my office. The **problem**

was my opportunity to remain centered and purposeful. I continued to keep my heart center open and to send forth free-flowing energy. Because of this, there was no fear in me. Fear is accompanied by tightness and shutting down. Fear is disempowering.

As they entered my office, I rose to help situate them in chairs. This movement of my body facilitated my determination to keep my energy flowing. I was **being the change I wanted to see happen**. I felt empowered, not only by a gesture that helped to establish that this was my turf, but also by the expansion in myself. The expansion through the heart center made room for them to express their anger.

I invited them to speak, to tell their sides of the altercation, and to express how they were feeling in this moment. All the while, I filled the room with unconditional love. I was **consciously creating a reality** of harmony. I kept the channels open so that there was room for their frustrations. I knew I was in charge, and that I could guide and encourage them. I was in a state of love. I was a powerful facilitator of the ongoing dynamic. The more I functioned in this way, the more respect the four of them afforded me.

In the end, all four of them softened, and the two girls left together in deep conversation about a project they had chosen as a joint effort. When their mothers left, they were calm and no longer focused on the incident.

As for me, I saw without doubt the healing effects of love and the power there is in choosing to love unconditionally, to keep the energy flowing. Having the **Love Principles** in the forefront of my consciousness enabled me to do this. My previous modes of functioning in threatening scenes were so radically different; it was as if I was not the same person. It wasn't just that I handled myself better or that I was more mature. I had had a spiritual breakthrough. It was as if I had broken through a shell into a new order of human being. I had taken an evolutionary step in that I could see the whole in which an event was occurring rather than being confined to my own perspective. It reminded me of how the human race moved from seeing only in black and white to being able to perceive color.

   Looking out past myself to my fellow human beings, I could see that the world would be a completely different environment if millions of people took the same rudimentary yet giant steps. We could become a people who are open to each other, who are unconditionally responsive, and who are aware that no one is separate and isolated from anyone else. We would know that what happens to any one of us happens to all of us, and that life is a constant opportunity to treat others with tender regard.

   The **Love Principles**, though simply stated, are profound in their import when they are lived. Embodying them requires commitment and practice. It is not enough to talk about them as good ideas because that doesn't change anything. Nor does it work to try to get others to do them in place of doing them ourselves.

   I remember an incident with a friend when I thought I was practicing **be the change you want to see happen instead of trying to change anyone else.** I wanted the friend to call me more often. In order to be the change myself, I called with regularity and made suggestions of things we could do together. The only thing that really changed was that I was now calling with more frequency. My friend never got the message that I wanted her to call more often.

   When I found myself growing frustrated and annoyed, I saw that I was trying to get my friend to be the change I wanted to see happen, instead of just being it myself. It was my **expectation** that caused me grief. To reiterate, the principles are to be lived, not expected as behavior from others. When I am not living them, it is easy to see that I am not being loving, that I am not functioning with full consciousness, and that I cannot possibly be powerful in the midst of a life circumstance.

* * *

As I present these profound principles, it is important to view them as one sentence divided into six equal parts. One without the others is more of a platitude than a source of power. It is only when we embody **all six of the Love Principles** in the same moment that remarkable dynamics occur.

A perfect example of this occurred in 1972 when I faced the problem of divorce from my husband of eight years. The problem was the pain that both of us experienced in coming to the decision. Throughout the wrenching months, I kept my focus on the **opportunity** the **problem** represented. I was choosing to **create a new reality** in which I would share my love energy in a life of service rather than focusing it all on a single individual. I was **being the change I wanted to see happen** in my own life, even though that meant causing pain to my husband who wanted our marriage to continue as it had been.

There were many exchanges in which he was not very kind because he was desperate to keep our relationship in tact. In those moments, I was tested in my ability to **receive him as beautiful exactly as he**

was. I could understand what was going on with him, but that did not lessen the pain. I needed the support of friends, but I was not very good at asking. It was during this period that I learned a great deal about **providing others with opportunities to give**. I used to pride myself on doing everything by and for myself, and not needing anyone. In this circumstance, the pain was so great that I needed to learn how to reach out and how to receive. I learned that **providing others with opportunities to give** was a way of loving others while also loving myself.

The biggest test came after our separation and divorce. His anger continued and he refused to have any contact with me for several years. I had hoped we could remain friends.

I kept the flow of my love open and held him in my heart during the time there was no contact, **receiving him as beautiful exactly as he was**. But my greatest saving grace was that I had **no expectations but rather abundant expectancy**. I held the hope that the anger would eventually diminish and that love would once again flow between us. I didn't know if or how that would ever be true. It might never have happened, but at least I made sure that the love energy continued to flow from me to him.

After several years, I received a letter from him. He wrote that his pain had diminished with the years and that he wanted me to know how grateful he was that I had been in his life. He told me that he had learned about love from me and that he wanted to thank me.

His letter surpassed any expectations I might have held and it opened the door to communication between us. The timing of the letter was perfect. A month later he suffered a heart attack and because a relationship had been re-established, I could be there for him.

During the remaining years of his life, we golfed together once a week. Though it was not appropriate for us to be together as marriage partners, it was clear every time we looked into each other's eyes that the great love we had shared was unshakable. He had always signed his little notes to me during our marriage, "Love unto Eternity." It remained true.

I credit the **Love Principles** for my ability to make it through the divorce, the time of no contact, and the re-uniting in a new form. Using all of the principles at once, I was able to keep my energy flowing and my heart open, even in the most trying of times. No matter how great the **problem**, I always knew that there was an **opportunity** there for me and it was my job to find it. When I would start to feel sorry for myself, I would remind myself that that was a reality creation and that I could make a new choice.

The easiest part was **being the change I wanted to see happen** because even when he had removed himself from my life totally, I was still able to send love to him. I **received him as beautiful** and held him in my heart. When I needed reassurance, I **provided others with opportunities to give** to me. But most of all, I had **no expectations** that I would ever hear from him again. I never shut down the **expectancy,** but I never trapped myself into thinking that if I sent love to him he would come around.

When he reached to me, I was already in a state of wholeness. That was a key juncture. I had chosen to love him consciously. I had chosen to exercise creative jurisdiction over my personality expressions, my thoughts, and my feelings. As a result, I was powerful in the face of all circumstances. Whether he spoke with me or not, I never created hurt. Instead, I directed love energy toward him and that enabled me to remain strong and to keep my life force flowing. Because I did not need his validation to put me at peace, I could receive his offering of validation as a pure gift of himself. His reaching to me was a new beginning.

Living all the **Love Principles** simultaneously is conducive to transformation of self.

* * *

From time to time over the years, people have suggested changing the principles to make them easier to do. For example, some have wanted to say that problems eventually *become* opportunities. But the power is in this truth: the **problem** itself *is* **the opportunity**.

Other persons have tried to eliminate a principle or two. The most popular candidate for removal is **receive all people as beautiful exactly as they are**. Some argue this is impossible to do. Others assert that there are many people who are not at all beautiful and that any normal person would agree. The truth is that the heart of *unconditional love* lies precisely in this principle, difficult as it seems to do in the beginning.

To make the spiritual shift within self to which I am referring there can be no change in *The Love Principles*. The change must occur in the individual wishing to live them. The fault is not in the principles. The limitation is in the one struggling toward unconditional love.

After absorbing the material in this book and making an unshakable commitment to practice living the principles, I hope that the reader will break through to an emancipated way of functioning in the world. It is my wish that everyone might come to know, as I have, the *true nature* of love. To know this is to touch the deeper meaning of life itself.

HAVE NO EXPECTATIONS
BUT RATHER ABUNDANT EXPECTANCY

An expectation, while seeming harmless, is an example of blocked energy. When we harbor expectations, we cling to private mental pictures of what will happen. Or, worse yet, we demand that life unfold in a particular way. It is this very demand that keeps us from functioning in an open love flow. We impose our wants on an interaction and hold to an image of an outcome before the interchange ever has a chance to unfold.

Expectations are the leading cause of disappointment. The bigger they are, the more pain we are likely to cause ourselves, and the longer the letdown is likely to live in our psyches. I know from personal experience what I am talking about.

About 50 years ago, when I was 11 years old, I entered a coloring contest at a neighborhood theater. The first prize was a new red bicycle. I desired that bike more than life itself, and I had no question that I would win it. First of all, I wanted it and needed it more than anyone else. Secondly, I was great at coloring.

I went to the theater with my mother. I tried to get us seats on the aisle so that I would have easy access to the stage when they called my name, but we ended up in the middle of a center row. Eternal optimist that I was, I found a way to justify our seating. As I waited for them to get to the top prize announcement, I fantasized my need to slide past all the people in my row. This would lengthen the applause, giving me more time to savor my win. My hands and arms would be high in the air, waving to those behind me and to those in front who were turning to see this small, deserving winner. When I would finally make it to the aisle, I would break into a run for the stage and the eyes of those in the audience would tear up in their joy that someone who wanted this so much had won.

Finally, the big moment came. I moved to the very edge of my chair as the build-up continued. Just as my name was about to be announced, I couldn't stand it any longer. I leapt to my feet, threw my head back and my arms high. My mouth was open and ready to emit the loudest cheer anyone had ever heard, when in that same second, someone else's name was called. Someone else's name filled that huge theater. Someone else had won my bicycle.

I was devastated and inconsolable. I refused to believe that I had lost. Finally, I determined that the judges had made a mistake.

Until I was about 40, I could still feel twinges of pain when I thought of the error they made. That was 30 years of carrying the letdown born of an expectation. By now I feel tremendous compassion for that small child. If I learned anything from that day, it was that one could be indelibly disappointed as a result of having an expectation.

There is nothing wrong with looking to the future with hope, or having goals, or holding visions. When we lift our energy in expectancy of a wonderful future it helps us to meet life circumstances in a positive way.

When we function in expectancy we are open to whatever comes our way, looking for the opportunities and listening for what is being asked. This is how it is to function in a state of conscious love. Our energy is moving forward to meet what is coming and we continue to grow and evolve as we deal with what is in our path. However, if we reduce our enthusiasm and openness to specific expectations about how something is to turn out or come into being, we limit our options and often miss out on what is actually transpiring.

As that eager child in the movie theater, I would have been better off had I focused on expectancy rather than the expectation that I was going to win the bicycle. I would have done my best coloring and I would have experienced the joy of that as an accomplishment in itself. The satisfaction would have been tremendous, so much so that it would have been a completed transaction. I would have felt pride that I had done a fine coloring.

Win or lose, the joy I would have felt about my fine work would have remained unaffected. I might not have won the bicycle, but I could have given myself my own reward for my fine effort by saving enough to buy my own bicycle because of how much I now deserved it. Or, I might have been so pleased with my expression of talent that I committed to a career as an artist as a result.

When we have expectations, we box ourselves into a pathetically small range of possibilities. When embodying expectancy, all our options are open. This is empowering. Love, in its unconditional receptivity to all that is, enables us to reach into the unknown, into that which lies a breath away from becoming.

I have known the particular thrill of welcoming the unknown in new relationships. I don't yet know the other very well but something about him draws me. I am excited to discover who he is. I am inexplicably happy in his presence. He speaks and my heart appears to jump. I tingle all over. In part, this is because of what I awaken in myself in relation to him. But in greater part, the phenomenon is occurring because I am whirling about in the unusual, the unexpected, and the unknown without trying to control anything. I am open and eager to know more and to bring forth untried parts of myself. I am "in love," in a state of unblocked heart-center joy.

I have had the same experienced in life situations that are new to me. Visits to a foreign culture, a climb to a pinnacle, a sudden merging with nature, are all examples. I choose **abundant expectancy** and refrain from imposing any previously held contentions on the current moment. I am "in love" with the moment, asking it to commune with me, to fill me, to teach me. I don't tell "it" how it should be. I come with open heart and receive what there is for me to unearth. **Having no expectations** empowers me to discover something brand new. Each such find makes me more whole and allows me to become more than I was a moment before.

Consciousness enables us to make choices. The more choices we make, the larger the field of choices. Wonderfully, as the field of choices expands, our consciousness expands to meet it. As consciousness expands, we become more powerful beings. It is a glorious continuum that has us stretching and growing to align with the *more* we are becoming.

* * *

Personal relationships are often the source of our

greatest difficulties due to expectations. We need to discover how we disguise our expectations of others. A handy device is to check on the language we are using.

When we say, "I depend on you to . . ." we are really saying, "I expect that you will . . ." The result is often trouble in the form of potential disappointment. Human beings are not inanimate objects. They are unpredictable and changeable. What we can really depend on is that they may alter their previous behavior, or that they may not follow through on something. The most we can say is, "I depend on you and I have no idea what you will actually do."

The same is true when we trust another, or invest in another, or believe in another. We cannot know how the other will respond. When we **have no expectations**, we are practicing **receiving them as beautiful exactly as they are**.

This is a way of loving that is open-ended. It allows people not only to be who they are but also who they are becoming. This is unconditional love.

It would appear that this would lead to chaos, but each individual is an equal part of the process. About the most we can do is hold ourselves accountable to our own choices. We can trust others to do or say something. However, whatever they do or say is their choice. They do not act because we depend on them to follow through.

People in relationship contract with each other in the same way an employer does with employees. The employees choose to fill the obligations of the position and the employer can depend on them to meet those obligations. At least, until the time they don't. In relationships we never know when that time is coming. If we have an expectation that all will be as we have always known it, we will not only be let down, we will have denied the nature of life itself. In fact, as the years go by, we may find ourselves wishing that our partners would not remain as we have always known them. We may begin to long for variety and unpredictability.

Relationship is an interaction, a live dynamic that is constantly becoming what it is. In that sense, it is not reliable.

One of the most important people in my life was a friend of over thirty-five years who served as my spiritual teacher. We were very different personalities and our needs in no way matched. This led to many ups and downs in our years of interacting. Nonetheless, we were able to retain a relationship of deep love.

Upon my return from an exciting four-month journey to Europe, I called, to reconnect. I was met with coldness on the other end of the line. The gist of the cryptic conversation was that my friend had chosen to be reclusive and wanted no further contact with me, or anyone else for that matter.

While I knew that the state of relationship is not reliable, I was shocked by this turn of events. It was a long time before I recovered, because in some small part of myself I clung to the unacknowledged expectation that the phone would ring one day and things would be as they had been. In my expectation, I was disempowered. The longer I hoped, the more I suffered. The more I convinced myself that she would call, the more I deluded myself. I told myself that I loved her and that that was why I would not let go of my desire. However, I was not really in a state of love. I was in a state of want. Love is unblocked heart center energy. My energy was blocked in solar plexus longing. I was not loving her so much as I was waiting for her to come around.

In the case of my husband, I am reminded that he had hoped that things between us would return to what they had been. It would seem we take turns holding expectations that disempower us.

My friend, my spiritual teacher, never did reestablish communication with me. Nor did she allow any communication from me to her. I practiced letting go and was quite successful until I saw that I still looked for ways to open the closed door. Years later, I discovered that my friend, my spiritual teacher, had actually lied to me. She was in communication with others even though she had defined herself as a recluse. Close mutual friends were in communication with her by both letter and telephone.

This news stirred anger in me. At first, I convinced myself I was angry with my friend. She had lied, after all.

Then I breathed. I remembered all **The Love Principles**. I didn't want to remember them. My real anger was that I had held on to the expectation that my friend would respond to me. I was angry because I did not get my way. I had done myself in with expectations one more time. Just because I want and need something does not mean I am going to get it. The more I demand it, the more disappointed I am likely to be. While I can exercise creative jurisdiction over my own life and action, I can never control another person's choices.

Too often, we try to play God in relationships by creating others in our image of how they should be. The most simplistic form of this is labeling and defining. A daughter is supposed to. . . If she doesn't, she has not met the mother's "rightful" expectations.

There is an even more complex form of creating

others in our image. It has to do with projecting onto another what we are seeking. For example, we choose someone as the object of our love and say that he is generous, loving, reliable, strong, etc. In fact, he may have exhibited these qualities at one time or another. But is he only this? Maybe not, except in our own eyes where we have locked him into an image.

As the beholder, we have taken this changeable, unpredictable, unique entity and locked him into a description we expect him to live up to. Inevitably the day will come when he will not be reliable or strong. We will be shocked. We will say that he is not the person we have always known. (Ah, but did that person ever exist?) We will beat our chests over how he has changed. We might become cynical and say that we will not trust anyone again. We might feel betrayed. And we have been. But, in truth, we have been betrayed by ourselves. Our daily focus was not on discovering who he was, and who he was becoming. It was on retaining the image we had created.

Though I have stated this hypothetically, I speak here as one who is so highly proficient at this useless skill that I could be called a master.

I once needed someone to be motherly, kind, gentle, affectionate and consistent. I chose a person who certainly could embody all those qualities and who often did. My flaw was that I expected her to be them all the time, and to always exhibit them in relation to me. She didn't. Did that deter me? No. I made excuses for the times she fell from grace: she was tired; she was dealing with difficult problems, etc. I continued to see her through rose-colored glasses. I was heading for a crash-landing with truth. When it came, and it had to, I was crushed.

In fact, she not only turned out to be terribly human, but she was inconsistent and untruthful when convenient. She used people and was bitchy. She could turn from kitten to tiger in a flash. She had exhibited these very qualities during the time I had placed and held her on her pedestal. When she did it in relation to others, I found good reason for her resorting to such behavior. In the back of my awareness, I knew full well that what she could do to someone else she could do to me, but I dared not acknowledge that fully. It would interfere with the image I had created. Alas, my knowing proved true and she did to me what she had done to others.

What I have described is not an isolated case. I am a very slow learner. I went through more than a dozen significant relationships over two decades in which I created a near-perfect person out of the person who was actually there. Each time, I was walloped by reality. Each time, my expectations were not met. Each time, I was disempowered by the expectations I held.

The great lesson I learned is to create in myself what I seek in others. My needs will then be met much more directly.

I needed to be treated with kindness, gentleness and affection. Since I stopped looking for these outside of myself I have been able to be kind, gentle and affectionate with myself! I have stopped being so hard on myself, so demanding. When I do something wrong, I awaken kindness through forgiveness. When I crave affection, I treat my body to a massage, or to physical activities that bring pleasure. I have learned not to push myself and am therefore gentler in my projections of what I can and cannot do in a given day.

More wonderful than anything is that I know how

to be consistent. I don't reach a hand to myself and then withdraw it because my mood has changed. Because I love myself more consciously, I am present to my needs as they emerge. I am unconditional in meeting them. I don't force myself to wait a week while I finish a work project. Nor do I berate myself for having needs.

As a result of being available to myself, on call 24 hours a day, I am much less dependent on others and I have ceased suffering the pangs of longing. I happily invite others into my life, but I am no longer dependent on them for my fulfillment or my happiness. This is healing love expressed toward self by self. It not only makes me happier but it places less burden on others in my life.

* * *

Many currently popular life-improvement techniques use visualization. The practitioner is told to see precisely what she wants and to hold the image of that firmly in mind. Eventually, if the focus is faithful enough and long enough, the car that she envisions will become a reality, right down to the exact color and hubcap design.

Some people who practice visualization get what they want; others don't. When they don't, it is easy to say that they didn't want it strongly enough, or that they weren't as focused as they might have been, or that they were simply not good at the technique. I would give still another explanation: visualization is not what it's touted to be!

We are all interconnected and interrelated, not only with each other but also with how life unfolds. We are not the sole determiners of the future or our wish fulfillment. We are participants in a larger whole and therefore subject to dynamics that exceed our individual desires, and especially any imposition of our will.

In light of this, it is easy to see that when I visualize and the reality results, it is more because I am in alignment with what actually is than because I caused it to happen. I am not suggesting that occurrences are predestined and that I don't have an active role to play in what emerges. Instead, I am pointing to the cooperative nature of the life process. I, for one, am glad that cooperative nature exists.

If we were able to receive or achieve everything we thought of, we might bring very disharmonious things into our lives. Then we would need to invest our life energy in disengaging, healing and restructuring. As part of a large whole, we are subject to a system of checks and balances.

Instead of visualizing a specific something we want, we function with greater power if we turn our attention to a larger perspective. This includes looking at the larger picture of our lives and how this desired object would fit in with our life purpose and our objectives for this over-arching time period.

The larger perspective also causes us to relate to ourselves as whole persons rather than seeking to meet the needs of only one component of self. Our minds might be filled with great ideas but these might not be in accord with the needs of our bodies. Or, we might seek to bring gratification to our bodies and cause disharmony in the spiritual component of self.

For years I had a desire for a Mercedes convertible. I could see myself proudly cruising around town with the top down. I could more easily envision me in the driver's seat than I could see myself coming up with the

$50,000 it would take to buy the Mercedes. The car was so expensive that it became a perfect opportunity for me to embrace the desire from a larger perspective, and to take my whole self into account.

First, I needed to expand beyond the Mercedes desire, and then beyond even wanting an automobile. Reflecting from the vantage point of the whole self, I looked at fulfilling my need for convenient transportation.

This was the beginning of stretching my perspective.

Having done this first step, I again asked myself, what do I really want? Each asking took me closer to the truth. I engaged in a process of empowering myself through conscious loving. I did this by moving beyond my expectation that I had to have a Mercedes to make me happy, and by opening my heart center. I breathed and allowed my life energy to flow as I gave myself my full, undivided attention during the exploration.

What I really wanted was to move about easily and without restriction and to remove hassles from my life such as constantly needing to repair my "old heap." And, if I was to have a vehicle, I wanted it to look good and I wanted to look good in it.

I continued to stretch. Even more than moving about easily, what I truly wanted was to make important contributions in my work. In order to do that, I needed to free my time and my energy for that purpose. Having a fine car would facilitate this.

Once I got to this stage, I looked beyond the vehicle I wanted to drive, to the "vehicle" I had chosen as a job or work expression, and beyond that to the vehicle of my creativity (my spirit, mind and body). By this stage of the process I felt exhilarated. I consciously loved myself by taking the whole of me into account.

When working with this as my vision, my images went beyond a specific make of car. My need for a better means of transportation remained, but the "transportation" now referred to the movement of talents and contributions, not just a conveyance from one location to another.

As a result of visualizing myself as a complete person, I discovered that I really yearned for a way to "cover more ground" in what I had to offer. I began wondering if I needed to move to another location, or reformat my work, or focus on improving my job status and income so that I was "more mobile" in relation to the unique gifts of self I had to offer.

Major changes did result. My partner and I decide to focus less on one-shot weekend workshops and more on developing intensives of longer duration so that participants could have programs in which to do long term spiritual work. The new level of work led to higher income and a more selective outreach. Our work took on deeper meaning for us and for those who participated.

Had I limited myself to an expectation of a Mercedes convertible, I would not have allowed myself to touch my greater desire for increased mobility within my work. I might have wished for the car, gotten it, and never turned my attention to the potential in myself that was really crying out to be met.

By reaching to the larger perspective and having **abundant expectancy**, I might have *also* **created the reality** of a breathtaking new Mercedes. There was room within the broader view for this smaller heart's desire, but within the more limited realm of well-defined expectations, there might not have been cognizance of the greater purpose to which my soul was calling me.

Having been enriched by the important insights

that came as a result of my process, I wondered if the convertible was still a part of the larger vision I was holding. I asked myself if it was in harmony for me to have this or to seek this? The answer to this question would allow me to align with what was appropriate to my greater good.

I knew that it would be in harmony if the purchase would not be a hardship, if it suited my driving needs, and if it was filling a desire I had held in my consciousness for a very long time. I knew that if I was contemplating the purchase in order to impress others and it was beyond my means, I would be doing myself a disservice and paying a steep price for creating an image.

I watched myself play with the idea that it was appropriate for me to entertain the desire even if my reason for wanting it was simply pleasure. This did not last long because I immediately had to confront how I would bring this into my life. What would I have to do to **create this reality**? I couldn't expect it to drop out of the "visualization sky," or magically appear.

To **create the reality** of a Mercedes convertible, I would have had to put myself in financial distress. That was not in accord with other values I held and I considered it out of the question.

I gave up on the desire that I could now see was more of a fantasy. A quick perusal of my consciousness showed me that I still wanted a convertible, but not necessarily a Mercedes. I began looking at used cars in mint condition and found a bright red Fiat that made my heart sing. It cost me $4,500 and ran perfectly. While it was a far cry from the Mercedes, it met my needs on many levels and made me very happy. I had my convertible without bringing stress and distress into my financial life.

The whole process had provided with me with profound learning, an expansion of my awareness, and, a delightful convertible as well. Three years later, thanks to the expanded work scene and active participation in the intensives, I was able to purchase a $15,000, top of the line, Chrysler convertible. Living in **abundant expectancy** empowered me to achieve an important learning about my work, and myself and, to acquire a very classy convertible. I had been functioning in very powerful love energy because I in no way locked myself into any one particular expectation. Instead, I placed myself in the flow, remained open to what was emerging and what was in harmony for me, and the result was complete satisfaction.

* * *

Having **abundant expectancy** acknowledges the unpredictable nature of life. It causes us to sit on the edge of each unfolding moment and readies us to jump up to meet what is being asked of us or what we are about to discover. In contrast, when we live with expectations, we tend to think that we know everything that is going to happen or to be said. If something different occurs, we might not see it or hear it because we are looking or listening through the filter of our own private world expectations.

This kind of behavior often occurs in familiar scenes such as a family visit. At Christmas we make the long journey home to the family nest. Our siblings and their offspring appear in the scene and our parents preside as if no time has intervened since the last such gathering. It really doesn't matter what we say or do in such a scene because no one is paying attention to us.

Instead, they focus on what they expect of us. If we function with expectations, we are guilty of the same thing in relation to our relatives.

We have all categorized each other and when any one of us opens our mouth to speak, we all hear what is being said in the framework of what we were anticipating. When we do this, we do not love each other because we are not open to each other. We block our energy flow because we are relating to an image inside ourselves and not to our actual relatives. It's much like going to visit someone but never going through the door after it has been opened. We stand outside and converse with our memory of whom we went to visit.

In a family visit it doesn't matter if we say something radically different from things we might have said in the past. The family instantly translates what we say to fit who we are supposed to be.

If we want to be seen in our new personas, and in addition we have expectations about how the family will react, we will soon be very discouraged. After a while, we too will succumb to the pattern and have expectations ourselves in relation to our family. In the end, none of us really needed to be there because the invitations really went out to who everyone used to be.

Through **abundant expectancy**, there is a way to change this dynamic. The expectancy would be in relation to us as well as to our relatives. Our focus would be on embodying the new we have become, not on whether they would see it or how they would respond to us.

Living in **abundant expectancy**, we are alert to what is coming in from outside stimulants so that we, ourselves, might respond freshly to them. We breathe before we speak, as if to ask ourselves "what is there for me to say that is different from how I have always responded in the past?" We seek to surprise ourselves; to wake ourselves up; to live as if we are really alive in this moment. All too often, when dwelling within the confines of expectations, we sound like clones of ourselves. We don't even need to be present because we can count on ourselves to utter the appropriate cliché in the appropriate moment.

We can experience great success if we hold the objective, "to be true to ourselves." To achieve this objective, we hold our focus on how we are presenting ourselves instead of how we are being received. If no one in the family sees the new us, our mission can be completely accomplished if we have acknowledged ourselves and stayed consistent with who we have become. When our focus is on fulfilling this objective, others cannot disappoint us.

* * *

Expectations are born in the mind. The mind is a file cabinet of how our lives have been in the past and of all our previous responses. The expectations are enhanced by our personal opinions of how things should be.

For example, if I am a good friend who calls another to sustain the relationship between us, I expect my friend to do the same. I say it is the way things are supposed to be. Why? Because I do them that way. Because I value sustaining relationships.

One of the problems here is the application of the tarnished Golden Rule: I do unto others as I expect them to do to me. I am setting myself up for pain. In the first place, my friend might not do things the way I do them at all. Secondly, my friend might not even like being done to as I do. By my very action, I might alienate my friend.

He might not like being called by me as often as I call. He might never call me because it is not his style, or because he might not want to encourage me to call.

Better would be to do unto others what pleases them, and to do unto myself what I value. The easiest way for me to know what pleases another is to ask. Then, if what he likes also pleases me, I can go ahead and do that. In this way, I do what I value and I also do what he values. The proviso is that I am functioning with no expectations that what pleases me will also please him.

In my early 20's I did what I thought was a grand deed. Some friends of mine were having a difficult financial time and I thought it would be kind to send them a special food treat. I bought up an array of gourmet delicacies such as caviar, smoked clams, pate, and baby shrimp. I packed a large box full and sent it off to them. I knew they would be thrilled, because I would have been if someone had made such an effort for me. My friends turned out to be animal-rights vegetarians and they gasped at what I had purchased. It was all they could do to get it out of their house. I was told later, "We seem always to have to clean up after you." I winced.

Nothing is apt to be as we expect it to be. Because we think something should be a certain way is one of the least likely reasons that it will be. Our assessment of the world and life is based solely on our random, isolated, and very limited experiences. The conclusions we draw can only be narrow. The proof is in how many thousands of times we encounter others who have completely different experiences and therefore radically different assessments.

To ask another what would please him and then to give it to him if it also pleases us and is in harmony for us to give, is to practice being conscious in relationship. In this way, we keep up to date with the other and with self. Our love is an expression of what brings joy to both of us. There is tremendous power in this because it is gratifying and satisfying to the two parties involved.

* * *

Goals should not be confused with expectations. A goal is a long-range view. It is something for which to strive and it serves to keep us on a specific course. While we hold the goal in our awareness, and even plan for how it will be accomplished, if we function in **abundant expectancy** we are constantly on the alert for how the goal can best be met. By not limiting ourselves to expected means, we open ourselves to a fertile range of possibilities. We are also ready and able to shift and change as necessary in relation to how life itself is influencing the unfolding of the goal. We are active participants but we do not demand that things happen in a particular way.

We are holding the goal in what is known as the Fertile Void. In the void, all things are possible in the midst of seeming emptiness. There is no past and no future. There is only the present moment, which does not exist because in the moment we are cognizant of it, it becomes the past.

In the Void, we are open to everything and we know no limits. There are no such things as "You have to," "You should," "You can't." There are no old tapes of discouragement. In the Void there is pure potential. When we stand in the Void with awareness of our goals, we look to see what more we can awaken in ourselves to better meet the tasks we have assigned ourselves. We stand empty in order to be filled anew. Because we are open to any possibility, we have a better chance than ever of reaching the goal and beyond.

When I was a child boxed in by apartment buildings that allowed only small glimpses of the sky, I dreamed of flying in the·airplanes that passed far above the rooftops. My goal was to have a life of travel. My expectation was that the career I was choosing, to be an actor in the theater, would enable me to meet this goal. As it turned out, most of my professional theater work was in New York. My career did lead to the taking of my very first flight, to Dallas, Texas, to do a beer commercial. But, the bulk of the work kept me grounded in the Big Apple.

The goal of travel, while no longer pressing, remained in my consciousness as I pursued expressions of meaning in my life. I relegated the goal to the Void and focused on my life purpose. Way led to way and by my early 30's, because being an actor was not filling my spiritual focus of functioning more consciously and creatively, I left the theater and New York to make a contribution through the dissemination of **The Love Principles**. Before long, a new pathway opened before me in the form of my current partnership with Diane K. Pike. As our work unfolded, I was on my way to Amsterdam, Israel, Jordan and Egypt, and I was criss-crossing our continent so often that I had little time to light in-between.

My goal, which had rested in the Void while I got my life and priorities into a new order, was realized. It continues to this day as I sit making revisions in this manuscript aboard an American Airlines flight to New York City.

* * *

Having no expectations but rather abundant expectancy prepares us to meet life as it is occurring, not as we demand it should be. When we live this way we look at what actually is, welcome it, stretch to meet it, and watch ourselves evolve in the process.

Releasing expectations is letting go; it is looking and asking and waiting and receiving. In that sense, it is to love consciously. Releasing expectations is discovering everything all the time as new and fresh. It is to regain the wonder of early childhood. It is to be surprised, delighted, challenged, stimulated, and enticed by life as it is unfolding. Thus, it is to be empowered.

Imagine if we were to wake every morning and look at the life partner beside us as if for the very first time. Imagine if we were to ask every single morning who this person is, what this person is becoming, what he or she means to us, and what we have to bring to this other? Imagine looking at ourselves that way every single morning. Imagine filling ourselves with gratitude for what has been, and awakening excitement about what is to come, and having absolutely no idea what might be! Imagine living in expectancy and therefore being fully prepared to meet anything and everything that comes our way.

To live this way is to have a constant love affair with life. Every moment becomes a stretch and an invitation to the more and the new. Heart center energy is flowing unconditionally and we are free from any restriction. We are evolving in each new moment and climbing to new heights of possibility.

* * *

To eliminate expectations is to remove blocks that stifle the life process. We are announcing that we are open to receive and to deal with all that comes to us. We are meeting our emerging destiny unconditionally.

We expand our capacity to love through the conscious choice to rid ourselves of limiting views of interactions with others. We make room in ourselves for persons who are very different from us and in so doing we, ourselves, change and grow. Every unique expression of life becomes yet another possibility for us, whether we choose it or not. Our capacity to love expands because we have extended to welcome variety and the unfamiliar.

We meet circumstances as they are and willingly explore our opportunities for growth. This keeps our life force flowing, prevents stress and eventual illness, and fills us with a steady glow of quiet joy. We become more expansive if only because we do not stop ourselves from fulfilling our ever-increasing potential.

Love is unblocked energy dynamically expressed in **abundant expectancy**. Openness, accompanied by eager enthusiasm for the unexpected, makes for an empowered interaction with each unfolding moment.

We are always more able to love another, and be loved by another, when the two of us unite without preconceptions, without encumbering past histories, and without anticipating anything.

*Practicing **The Love Principles** in each moment enables us to be alert to what is transpiring, and excited about the unknown that is about to be revealed as a result of mutual risking.*

* * *

Exercises for Practice:

1. View the significant other in your life as if you were seeing him/her for the very first time. Notice each day what you have not seen or appreciated, or what has changed. Do this every day for a week.

2. Choose a desire you have and look beyond it to *the more* you really need and want. Explore how you can give it to yourself right now, through the resources at hand and through changes you might make.

3. In a conversation with someone with whom you interact frequently, listen with **abundant expectancy** and allow yourself to make spontaneous, unpredictable responses. Tell this person what you believe to be true of him or her and ask if your perceptions are valid. As the person responds, open yourself, with **no expectations,** to experience his/her reality.

PROBLEMS ARE OPPORTUNITIES

Rarely a day goes by when we are not stymied in some way. No matter how we organize ourselves, it is inevitable that something will go wrong. We are faced with a problem. Some problems are small, others seemingly insurmountable. But all problems have one truth in common. **Every problem is an opportunity.**

A problem is a block. It stops us from proceeding. It is like a stone wall that suddenly appears in our way, especially when we are in a hurry. Problems are inconvenient, annoying, and bothersome. They are uninvited detours that interfere with our lives. They are pesky, in that they demand attention and draw us away from what we thought we needed to focus on.

Every problem, whether minute or overwhelming, **is an opportunity**. It is not that the problem eventually *becomes* an opportunity once we figure out how to resolve it. It is that the very problem itself is the opportunity that is presenting itself to us. If we meet a problem with resistance, we are not functioning in love. We are not open to what the problem is offering and because we are blocked, we cannot and will not interact with it. We are stuck. We may blame our immobility on the problem, but we have disempowered ourselves by cutting off our live-giving force.

On May 13, 1968, at the age of 29, I was stricken with heart disease. The ride to the hospital in the middle of the night was horrendous. I was suffering chest and shoulder pains and I could not breathe. I did not know what was happening to me.

By the next day, as I sat in the cardiologist's office, I had dismissed the event as psychosomatic. I was disturbed that I was missing a day of teaching. I was feeling a little better and looked forward to returning to work the next day. Then the problem hit.

I was diagnosed with viral pericarditis. The cardiologist, a kindly, white-haired, solemn-faced fellow, told me I had a serious illness and that I would be in bed for about six weeks. I thought he was out of his mind.

I resisted his pronouncement. I expressed disbelief, argued, challenged, and refused. This problem was no opportunity for me. It was threatening to completely interfere with my lifestyle, my plans, my everything. I would have no part of it. He was wrong. And if not that, then this illness was wrong.

This is a familiar approach to problems: get rid of them at any cost. Ward them off as best we can. Marshal all our forces and counterattack. If there is no other solution, enter into outright denial. We might even be successful and push on with our agenda, but, in truth, we can do this for only so long. What usually happens is that the same problem presents itself again, and then again, until we are willing to look at what the opportunities are.

My outburst with the cardiologist lasted about ten minutes. It had taken all the remaining energy I had. I was not even aware I was expending it and that my resources were diminishing rapidly. My body began to collapse into itself. The experience was so powerful that it seemed to me I had become ill as a result of the doctor's diagnosis. He had given me the disease that was literally taking over my body as I sat in his office.

When I finished my tirade, I felt completely depleted. I could barely breathe. I could hardly move. It was as if a giant sucking machine had vacuumed the life out of me. I was so weak and incapacitated that I had no way of recognizing myself in the chair. It was then that I began to weep. I had finally faced the problem. I had allowed myself to feel fear and discouragement. This opened the way for me to feel compassion toward myself, and tenderness. I was beginning to move toward a state of love. Soon I would be able to know the opportunities that lay in the problem.

A key step in preparing to discover opportunities is: face the problem. Do not run from it or fight it. Look at it. Greet it. Meet it. If possible, welcome it. Receive it. Once we have done this, we have created a climate for insight and learning.

During the next six weeks, and it did take that long, I did not need to be forced into complete bed rest. I had no choice. I could barely move and needed the total care of my husband. It took all the strength I had to lift a comb up to my hair, but there was no way I could use it. I completely lost my appetite and dropped to 98 pounds. It took an eternity to walk to the bathroom, and hours to recuperate from the trip.

I had always been a warrior. No problem was too big for me. I fought against the best of them. If I didn't win, I would be clever enough to find my way around what stopped me and take another route to the same destination. I brought up my tough side whenever anything stood in my way. I knew nothing about **opportunities in problems**. Problems were the enemy and I would never surrender.

The heart disease was a new challenge because I couldn't fight. I did not even have the energy to mentally argue. I was a complete prisoner.

My confinement was my learning chamber.

Step One: *Move from Demanding to Questioning*.

This is an excellent means of discovering opportunities. I did not have the energy to demand that the problem go away or that my life be returned to the way it had been.

My first questions were rudimentary and not very helpful because they were "why" questions. Why was this happening to me? This is not an opportunity-oriented question if it is offered as a whine or a complaint.

"Why" questions invite answers from the mind rather than the intuition. The only thing the mind has to work with is old data that I entered in the first place, and most of that was made up of irrelevant thoughts and opinions.

Step Two: *Enlist the Intuition*.

Intuition invites insight and leads to deep knowing. I needed to ask "what" questions rather than "why" questions. I knew the illness was not a random occurrence. It meant something that I had been stopped. What was the meaning of the pericarditis? It had something to do with the heart, but all I knew at that time was that it was a physical problem. I knew nothing of the heart chakra, that this might be an opening of that powerful energy center.

Was I trying to tell myself something important? What was it? I had little energy and could not function as I had been. I was clearly sending a message to myself that I needed to change my lifestyle, my pace, and my priorities.

What was I asking of myself? I did not know and I was too weary to find out.

Step Three: *Wait*.

There is never only one answer to any of these questions. The answers unfold. As each dimension is touched, more knowing is uncovered and more questions are asked. The opportunities are manifold and continuing.

The first thing I asked of myself was that I become aware that a way of life was ending for me. I could no longer go on as I had been. To understand more, I had to wait. A major shift was in process and it was for me to discover what new shape my life was going to take and what I would need to guide that process.

Step Four: *Change*.

A problem doesn't really stop us; it starts us in a new direction.

This was certainly true for me, although I did not know what the new direction was at the time. Transformation does not occur suddenly. It takes place over time and is facilitated by the small but significant changes that need to be made along the way.

I could no longer take simple tasks for granted. Everything I did required my concentration and full attention. I am speaking of the smallest things, such lifting a pencil, listening to a sentence, or wiping my brow. Every second of life and every interaction with it became precious to me, and evoked my deep appreciation. Before this I had always taken life for granted, as well as my abilities to function at will. Now, because every action took so much energy and was such an accomplishment, I was overcome with gratitude at every small feat. Life itself was becoming a worship service. I began offering praise and thanksgiving for being alive. I had consciously chosen to live in a state of love.

As large and as life threatening as this problem was, it was equally a life-transforming opportunity. Because I could no longer take anything for granted, I began to marvel at everything. I was no longer driven. I became aware of feeling love for no one in particular but for everyone and everything in general and even for strangers. The new sense of love I was experiencing, a universal love, had its origins in my great sense of gratitude. Commonplace events were like miracles to me.

When I began to regain my strength, my husband and I went to dinner in Greenwich Village one evening. My appetite had improved a little and just being out was incredibly special. My only other excursions had been to the cardiologist. I remember most clearly the moment when we left the restaurant. There were three steps up to the sidewalk. They might well have been Mount Everest. It took me ten minutes to climb those three steps. It was the first time in my life I knew what real achievement was. I was graced with the blessing of a body well enough to follow through on what it was directed to do.

Following that day, I entered a six-month period of limited activity. Only after that could I turn my attention to rebuilding my muscular structure.

The heart disease was an opportunity to release my past and start afresh. The illness of the heart was the opening of my heart center to unconditional love. I could feel my capacity for love expanding. The way I loved began to change radically.

The opening of the heart center was an invitation to embark on a spiritual awakening. During my long recovery time, I was quieter. I actively listened to the intuitive side of myself and became conscious of an inner voice of wisdom. I had a sense that something hovered for me to discover. A breakthrough of some kind.

There had been similar opportunities in my earlier life, times when I had been stopped. But in those cases I had fought my way through. I developed a knee disease as a child that rendered me inactive for an entire summer, a devastating experience for an over-active child. Every day, as I sat with my knee elevated, I pushed from within myself to get well in order to get on with my agenda. If there had been a learning for me in being stopped, I missed it because I sought to overpower the circumstance with my will. There was little power in this.

In another instance, I was unable to attend daytime college upon graduation from high school. I determined I would get a degree anyway. I worked full-time and went to college four nights a week. While this had its admirable aspects, what I did not consider was that the obstructions to day college attendance might have been a clear invitation to me to pursue a career in the theater wholeheartedly and without distraction. I was convinced that I needed "something to fall back on," and that was my sole motivation for higher education. I have no idea how my life might have been different had I said a full "yes" to my schooling limitation and pursued a career in a daring way instead of insisting on going to college.

* * *

The problem is not the problem. The problem is the vehicle for something more, something new. It is the opportunity. What can really be called a problem is the resistance we put up, our unwillingness to seek the meaning of the problem. We are more the problem than any "it." If I had been willing to receive the heart disease at its onset I could have saved myself significant emotional grief. This might have facilitated the healing process and my learning would have commenced immediately. I would not have spent energy regretting that this had happened to me. I would not have further jarred my body with my angry response, which was a further attack upon myself.

When life interferes with our lives, we have a problem if we say "no" to the interference. If we say "yes," we have an opportunity. A problem is an opportunity to which we have said "no."

One way to monitor our responses in this regard is to check to see if our life energy is blocked or flowing. When we are locked into a problem, the energy is bound. When we move to pursuing opportunities, the energy flows freely.

I had a run-in with a fellow-worker. Although we were collaborating on a project, my partner leapt to make decisions on his own as if he were the only one involved. I experienced the problem as a direct hit to the solar plexus. I stopped breathing, created tension, and was generally "pushed out of shape." I knew I was locked into the problem because no energy was moving and I was unwilling to do anything about it. I stewed. I didn't want to take a breath because I did not want to open myself any further to the situation.

When locked into this mode, I was locked into inaction. I could not be creative, or even present. I certainly could not be loving, and I was feeling absolutely powerless. I felt like a child in the presence of a domineering adult.

A way to break free in such a situation is to move to a "what" question: What do I want? This is an excellent question because it puts us in touch with our feelings. The energy of feelings is powerful and can quickly enable us to move forward.

"I want to be taken into consideration," was my response. Phrased this way, I was still blocked because I wanted my partner to do something in relation to me: to take me into consideration. Obviously, I had no control over him and couldn't get him to agree or even to see my side of the issue.

Asking a question was not enough; neither was making a statement that held me in a weak position. I needed to speak directly, for myself.

I reminded myself that I was an equal. I deserved to have an equal say. I resolved not to stifle myself. I deserved respect and I would earn it by not holding back what there was for me to express.

I could act on that. I could move energy and therefore move to the opportunity level. First I affirmed that I was an equal. I no longer approached the situation by asking him why he did what he did. That was to put myself in a one-down position. Instead, I said straightforwardly, "The transaction was not clean because you did not have the benefit of my input. I propose we do . . . Let's make an appointment to explore this together so that we can proceed properly." The response to me was positive and the two of us were able to move on to the new, together and on equal footing.

I had clearly moved beyond the problem dimension of the event. My opportunities were manifold. I rediscovered my strength and reminded myself that thrusting myself into a child-parent configuration always handicaps me. I was reminded of the need to be prepared, to offer a balancing plan. I took this as an opportunity to practice respecting myself. I did this by asserting myself. The entire experience was a chance for me to test and affirm my strengths and to stand up in the full height of myself.

Interactions such as these are many and minor in the course of our lives. They are momentarily irritating and then they are forgotten. But they must be addressed.

Minor problems that go unattended aggregate. Eventually they gather in hidden places in self. One day, we gather one too many. The aggregation "hits the fan" and we explode. No one around us can understand our degree of rage, and neither can we if we have forgotten all the responses we have stored up regarding prior circumstances.

If we don't finally blow up, physical or emotional illness may result sometime down the road. If we are observant we can directly relate the dis-ease to the kind of avoidance we have been practicing. I have seen people with arthritis who have stiffened at the thought of ever changing their established ways of doing things. They have done this throughout their lives and it shows up in their bodies. If not stiffening, they have had rigid responses when they didn't get their way and their bodies reflect the rigidity. Others have hearing losses because for years they have not wanted to listen to what life has been saying to them.

The most classic case is a woman who did not

honor a spiritual awakening by pursuing it fully, and instead entered into a marriage as a way of getting free from her parents. Although her husband was a beautiful, caring being, she wanted out of the marriage for endless years but never acted on her own behalf. Then she lost her memory. The doctors had an appropriate diagnosis for her condition, but what seemed clear was that she had finally found a way out. She left her life because she could not or would not leave her marriage or honor her spiritual awakening.

In my own life, I discovered the role that control played in relation to troubles with my lower back. I wanted my life circumstances to fall out in particular ways. Every time they didn't, or when relational dynamics were frustrating and I could not control the outcome, I would create tension and grab hold in my lower back. I never realized I was doing it and I suffered horrendous pain because of it. I got no relief until I began to realize what I was doing, and I got no healing until I began to see that my opportunity was to move beyond my need to control. I needed to stop making demands on life; to stop adding to a storehouse of small angers, each of which lingered as tension in my body in the area of my lower back. All the while I thought my back was causing me to suffer and that that was the problem, my opportunity had been to discover that I was the cause of the suffering and my back was screaming to get my attention.

* * *

Focusing on the **opportunities in a problem**, rather than looking only for an immediate solution, leads to self-growth and to doors that are opening.

I remember receiving a letter in the mail from a people-worker whose practice was diminishing. She wrote insisting that those of us on her mailing list send her financial support. She threatened that if we did not sustain her, her vital work would not continue. The implication was that we would be responsible for causing this loss.

I was very taken aback by the demand. It seemed to me that she was missing the point. If her work was diminishing, perhaps the expression she had chosen was finished and this was an opportunity for her to move on to something new, something more dynamic and more worthy of her efforts. Her letter sought a solution to her immediate financial problem while her opportunities were clearly long range. She might have moved to work with a different clientele, or in a different location. She might have turned to writing what she had learned over the years and, as a result, found a whole new career in publishing.

In this example, the people-worker may have needed to let go of the form of her work, as she had known it. This is another important aspect of dealing with problems as opportunities. When something comes to an end, a way of functioning, a relationship, a job, a residence, or whatever, it is imperative to let go. There may be grief, which is a process of releasing, but to let go is to make room for what is to unfold.

Letting go opens a space for the unknown to germinate. My partner and I lived in San Diego, California for 21 years. Given that the climate was ideal and our house was on a hill that overlooked the Pacific Ocean, we never had a thought of moving. I used to joke that I was going to leave the house to myself in my will, and when I reincarnated, I would simply reclaim it.

Although we had behaved like typical Californians for two decades by ignoring earthquake threats, in our 21st year a number of factors began influencing us toward a move. First we began to feel it was time for some kind of change in our work. But more specifically, it was the early 1990's, a time of great change at the end of an astrological age. We began to have dreams of great upheavals on many levels and of enormous earthquakes. While we weren't frightened, we thought it prudent to be practical, and we turned our attention to relocating.

I cannot begin to describe what a problem this was. When we looked at the map of the United States we immediately eliminated 95% of it as a place to live. On the personality level, neither of us really wanted to move, let alone relocate to another city. We found more levels of resistance than we could have imagined. We experienced congestion in ourselves and knew that it was blocked life energy. We weren't responding in love to the change that was imminent. As long as we were not consciously choosing to go with the flow of the energy as it was, we could not know or benefit from the love force. We could not function with power. The clearest manifestation of this was that our house was not selling. We didn't want to let go and it wasn't going. We finally released our ambivalence and committed ourselves to change. Remarkably the contingency bid on our house turned into a sale within the week. It was a clear and positive example of unblocking the life force and allowing the future to emerge.

We opened the space for something new by letting go of the old. The new that flooded in was exceptional. We found our way to Scottsdale, Arizona, a beautiful environment with a tenth the population of San Diego and therefore less traffic, pollution and congestion. Our new community borders on Phoenix, so that we lost none of our cultural advantages and we still have easy access to a major airport. The money from the sale of the California home bought us a dream house in Arizona, complete with our own swimming pool and spa. Our home work environment was greatly enhanced in size and ambiance, and the joy we came to know we could never have predicted had we held on to our desire to stay put in San Diego.

The move to Arizona was a classic example of a **problem being an opportunity** even beyond dreams. My partner and I knew no one in the area of our relocation. We hoped we would not have to start all over again by making contacts and establishing ourselves in the community. Before we had a chance to worry about it, we were called by an acquaintance of long-standing who invited us to Iowa to work as consultants. This was a completely new area of work for us and led to our development of a new program called Leadership Mastery. Effortlessly, it seemed, we had stepped through a door as it opened.

Releasing has much to do with being willing to relinquish the control we think we have. Life is a cooperative venture and we are by no means the grand designer who determines how it should go.

* * *

One of the great difficulties with knowing that **problems are opportunities** is that we human beings cling to mental pictures of how things should be. When things do not meet our expectations, we become unnerved and upset. We begin to demand that life change to suit us. Then we are stuck in our own limited private worldview.

We make small advances. For example, in relation to a problem or two we look for the opportunities. When we find some, we move energy. We shift and change. And, we go on to tell others of the importance of looking at life this way.

Then, we confront a large problem and we freeze. We refuse to look at opportunities and dismiss anyone who has the audacity or insensitivity to remind us that we might. We want the problem to go away. We are unwilling to change. We take our stand against the great life inequity.

I took such a stand in a relationship. For many years, a friend played a very key role in my life. I loved her as much as I ever loved anyone. We were beside each other through several of life's joys and crises including my divorce, the long illness and demise of her husband, several painful incidents with her children, a relational crisis in my life, and her remarriage. It seemed this profound relationship would be in my life forever.

Long years into our friendship, she had held me tenderly as I sobbed over the death of my former husband and the great pain I experienced because his current wife did not inform me of his passing. Neither of us had any way to understand that, or so it seemed. Then, in a bizarre turn of events, when my dear friend's son, who was as a brother to me, died of AIDS, she, to my astonishment, never informed me. When I did learn of his death, I wrote a letter of sympathy to her and also expressed my despair over not having heard the news from her or from her current husband. There never was an answer to my letter.

This was a perfect circumstance for choosing a response that would either make this an insurmountable problem or a tremendous opportunity.

I could feel my solar plexus revving up for a "feeling field day": hurt, indignation, disbelief, anger. You name it, it was revving. It was easy for me to judge this as a clear case of betrayal, a great life inequity in relation to which I was unwilling to change or accept any responsibility. I felt I had been done a great wrong. It was so great that to overcome it, to see the opportunities, and to move beyond, I needed to acknowledge that I was dealing with more than a crisis. I was dealing with the essence of life itself, what I refer to it as "isness."

Everything in life simply is. It is not better or worse. It is!

I did not want to face that truth, but once I did, the opportunities not only became clear, they stuck out all over the place because of how many times in the past I had wrung myself out over relational entanglements.

I took a breath and let go. This is the way it is; this is the way she is. I released her. I really never had her in the first place. None of us do. In fact, I imposed an image upon her because I wanted someone to meet a particular set of needs. She joined me in the dynamic because she wanted to meet those needs for her own reasons.

I saw that there was no way for me to understand her behavior. My opportunity was to love without emotional entanglement. I blessed her on her way and expressed gratitude for what we had had. I breathed and let my love energy flow. I was loving consciously, and as a consequence, I was empowered to handle the blow of the termination of our friendship.

What could have been shattering for me was freeing. I learned that I could give of myself, and receive, and then let go and move on.

This was more than discovering the opportunity in a problem. This was a major life learning. My willingness to see it as it was and to embrace it has resulted in a profound transformation in my life. Remembering Martin Luther King's famous words at the Lincoln Memorial, I can affirm that I am truly free at last.

The phrase "that's the way it is" is quite true, but it is usually said more in resignation than as a statement of truth.

"What is" goes beyond any one of us, or even all of us. "What is" comes into being at the behest of something larger than all of us. "What is" is part of the unfolding of the unseen pattern. It is the result of a Greater Harmony than any of us can know. We can hold preferences in relation to what is, but how we think or feel or act does little to change what is.

What we do about "what is" determines whether we experience it as a problem or an opportunity. This is where our freedom of choice comes into play. We cannot impose our will on what is, but we can determine whether we will grab the brass ring in the circumstance or ride round and round in our own circular thinking.

* * *

One of the great tests of my life came when one of my most significant relationships was in jeopardy. For months I struggled against the circumstances and alternated between considering suicide or murder (though not seriously, I trust) as a solution. I was long into the despair before I remembered that only math problems have solutions. This was an opportunity for something.

I did not want to know what it was. In fact, I wanted to take all **The Love Principles** and do away with them because I was hurt and threatened.

My partner had made choices that were totally contrary to what I held to be inviolate and resulted in emotional wrenching that went on interminably. I tried every way I knew to make my partner change. I desperately wanted to continue in our relationship as it had been. The agonizing was unbearable.

I was blinded to what the opportunities might be because of the magnitude of my suffering. There seemed to be no move for me to make until the day I observed that my partner was on a path of self-destruction, on a journey into a form of hell. On that day I chose life rather than death for myself. Though the union was all-important to me, I would not also make the journey into the consuming fires. I was now dealing with matters of the life and death of my integrity, not just the relationship.

The day I became empowered was the day I yielded. I gave up fighting against life as it was presenting itself. Taking a deep breath, I touched "isness." I saw that I could make decisions only for myself, and once I began doing that, I felt disentangled and empowered. I became independent within the relationship. It would continue, or it would not. I was not in control of "it." I began making choices on my own behalf, and as I did, the heavy weight of the problem lifted. I had been crushing myself.

I made a choice *for me*, for what I needed in order to go on as a functioning human being.

My learning in this calamity was that my wholeness depended solely on me and not on my bonding with another. I discovered that I could survive if I had to go on alone. I was strong enough as an individual to deal with anything. In the end, the relationship lasted and was far better than ever before. That was how the pattern unfolded. Needless to say, I was very glad. But the truth is that there were other profound relationships in my life that ended in ways other than I wished. Oddly, I am equally glad. I have learned from both varieties, and grown, and been enriched.

Love, unblocked heart center energy, is born of valuing everything that happens. No moment of life is wasted because every moment carries the seed of an opportunity.

The essence of conscious loving is knowing that with every breath we take, we are blessed. To know this is actually to be blessed ealed. What might have been debilitating becomes invigorating instead, and we prepare ourselves to step consciously into the more that we are becoming.

* * *

A problem is an opportunity for the expression of gratitude. Difficulty comes and we welcome it with love, seeking the gifts it has brought to us. Every tribulation is an intersection.

To meet everything as an opportunity is to cherish life. It is to know that everything is for our benefit — for our learning and growth. This way of living is a choice.

* * *

Exercises for Practice:

1. When you hear yourself saying "No" to something or someone, or when your energy is congested because of an occurrence, stop, breathe, and ask, what are my opportunities here?

2. Look at a chronic problem in your life. Instead of demanding that it go away, or that your life return to a time prior to the problem, open your heart to your circumstance and embrace it with your full strength. Begin to act on what you see you **can** do right now. Move one little step at a time toward the new that is ready to emerge.

3. Each day, offer gratitude for something you consider a blessing in your life. Each day, offer gratitude, and mean it, for something you view as a problem. Remind yourself that every problem is blessing, an opportunity you haven't yet seen.

PROVIDE OTHERS WITH OPPORTUNITIES TO GIVE

The spiritual unfolding of the human being is delineated by a series of levels or developmental states. One stage we go through is identification with "the group." This is a tribal stage of development. We belong to the group but do not know ourselves as individuals within it. What the group does, we do; what it believes, we believe. The people within the group seem to move as one mass and are identifiable as "a people."

When we begin to individualize, we not only pull away from the group and its influence, we actually rebel in order to assert our independence and ourselves. A first step is that we begin to think of ourselves as separate. We no longer dress or behave as others do. Perhaps we break from the dominant religious traditions. We often move from the home area, preferably to a place where no one knows us or the place that we came from.

A weakness of this stage is that we, as individualizing beings, temporarily forget that we are part of a large whole which affects us and which we affect.

This stage lasts as long as is necessary for us to build strong egos through which to function. We become practiced at making choices, at following through on decisions, and at **creating our own reality consciously**.

The next stage is a return to the group. But this time, the interaction is very different. First, we do not return to identification with a personal group: a family, a tribe, a religious sect, a specific community, or a nationality. This time, we know self as part of the larger whole, as a vital and contributing part of humanity itself.

We are unique in our expressions rather than carbon copies of others. We are not impressed by, afraid of, or bound by doctrines promoted by established orders. We weigh and measure everything consciously and proceed with what is in harmony for our unfolding. We also acknowledge everyone else as unique. We value others and the gifts of self they contribute to the whole.

It is during this third stage of development that the **Love Principle provide others with opportunities to give** is practiced effectively. If we know that we are unique, then we know we have something special to contribute to the whole. We also know that we are never alone and that others around us can contribute significantly to us. We sense and identify a purpose for our lives and we begin to align our actions with it. As we simultaneously receive from others, we come to know that we are part of a grand design that is intricate, alive and emerging.

During this stage, we learn that life is a process of giving and receiving. There is great joy and reward in giving because we are blessing another. Equally, there is great joy in receiving because we bless others when we, in turn, **provide them with opportunities to give** of themselves. In fact, when we invite others to give to us, we acknowledge their worth and affirm their uniqueness. In this sense, when we ask another to give, and we receive, we actually give the giver a gift.

It is said that it is more blessed to give than to receive. While this may be true, what if everyone were to insist on giving? There would be no one around to receive.

We all enjoy the position of giving. Sometimes we even experience a small degree of superiority in this role. The receiver is needy, and we, from our position of abundance, are the caregivers. What we have to give, the other needs.

When people are constantly put in the position of being given to, their self-esteem erodes. They begin to feel like children in the midst of adults who look after them. Furthermore, no one asks them to contribute their gifts in return. An unhealthy cycle is set in motion, which not only continues throughout their lives but is also passed on to the next generation.

This is the very cycle that exists in welfare systems. While changes have been set in motion to transform this system, the changes are in the realm of contracts whereby the welfare recipient must get a job within a certain time period or lose benefits. What is missing in this approach is providing the recipients with the opportunity to give to others of their talents, knowledge, and life-experience during the time they are receiving benefits. If this were in place, the recipient would build a sense of self-worth and society itself would benefit.

* * *

Love in its highest form involves consciously interweaving our lives with others so that we know that we are part of a cooperative endeavor. It is here that we find our greater strength.

If I needed to lift a heavy object, I would be silly if I asked only one of the cells in my right hand to do the work. For the job of lifting, all the cells in my hands, arms, legs, back, etc. are needed to interact with one another, each making its unique contribution. Similarly, the whole to which we are contributing will be much stronger if we involve others in our projects and activities than if we try to do everything ourselves.

When we **provide others with opportunities to** give, we initiate a synergistic process in which the greater harmony is served because we break out of the one way (ours) and into many ways that emerge from joint effort. There is no way to predict what will come of the involvement of many differing viewpoints. The results are less planned and the richness and depth of what emerges often pleasantly surprises the participants.

During my teaching days, I served as Human Relations Coordinator at a high school. It was a time of great racial disturbances that led to unrest and sometimes violence. I wanted to design a show for presentation to the student body. Its purpose was to honor the school population's differences, confront stereotypes with humor, and bring the students to a commitment to mutual respect. While I had wonderful ideas and was able to write uproarious skits, I wanted to be sure that the students would fully relate to what I was creating. I pulled together a cross section of students and elicited their critiques.

As a result of their input, rewriting, and additions, the program took on much greater life. Many of the skits, while left intact in terms of content and message, were reworded to capture the way the students themselves would speak. This adjustment made a world of difference in how the program was received.

The contributing students also added dances popular with their peers, as well as movements and gestures that would stir the general assembly to recognition. The joint effort was much more comprehensive than what I had originally conceived.

The entire process was exemplary of the benefits of **providing others with opportunities to give** because it brought together a very diverse group of individuals who were focused on remaining open to each other, to their differences, and to a larger cooperative purpose. They came to know each other through creativity, and to value each other, as they never had before. They were not only giving to each other in ways they never had, they were receiving from each other and feeling richer for the exchange.

One of the key elements for me was that I expanded my boundaries. I opened myself to differences and allowed those differences to stir me and to break me out of my private world ideas about how things should be done.

True breakthroughs occur in a climate of cooperation in business or relationship or lifestyle.

* * *

Another example of the power of **providing others with opportunities to give** was my discovery of a whole new art form.

During a visit to a museum, I silently provided artists with the opportunity to give to me. I came upon a multi-media display that was so profound an idea to me that I experienced a paradigm shift in my image of myself as an artist.

The artist, like myself, had a great sense of color and was an excellent photographer. I had given up painting decades ago because I had little talent for drawing. I became a semi-professional photographer but could feel the longing every now and then to hold a brush to canvas. The artist before me had photographed beautiful scenes in black and white and then used acrylics and watercolors to shift the photo to an impressionistic painting. It was so beyond anything I had ever thought of doing, that I shouted out my joy in the gallery. I felt as if I had just been scooped up by a hot air balloon and flown into a world of new possibilities. I had provided the artist with the opportunity to give to me and my creative life was reawakened in that very moment.

* * *

When **providing others with opportunities to give** it is important that we hold **no expectations** *that* the other will give, *what* the other will give, or *how* the other will give. When we ask another, we invite an interpretation and an expression different from our own.

It is imperative, therefore, that we welcome what comes, that we are present to the expression, that we are open to explore how to incorporate what we are receiving. When we practice this principle we ask others to give to us of *their* reality, thereby enabling us to expand our own. This expansiveness, this openness is a way of consciously loving.

One of my favorite examples is in the realm of

pleasure. I asked a loved one to scratch my back. It seemed a simple enough request until I began receiving the gift that was being offered. The touch was far too heavy and it was localized as if to deal with an itch. What I had in mind, as surely anyone would know, was a light, feathery fingernail canvassing of the entire back for at least 15 minutes. I was disappointed. I was disappointed because I was holding very specific expectations.

In this instance it is very easy to see how all the **Love Principles** are one statement that is divided into six equal parts. If I **provide another with the opportunity to give** to me, I must be ready to receive in **abundant expectancy,** I must **receive the other as beautiful** in his or her chosen expression, and I must **consciously create the reality** of openness in order to perceive what comes to me as **an opportunity rather than a problem.** I am **being the change I want to see happen** by opening to receive. Therefore, my responsibility is to receive and not to try to change how the other gives.

In the case of the back scratching, my request needed to be stated more clearly. I was, in fact, not providing my loved one with an opportunity to give me just any old back scratch. I wanted something very specific. Under such circumstances, I have an obligation to detail my request so that the other has a chance to please me. By being specific, I consciously engage in a love exchange.

This is true in so many life areas; sex, for example. Excellent sexual expression does not come from hit and miss fumbling or from groping around to satisfaction. It derives from two adult lovers discussing their needs and wants and even training one another in acts of pleasuring. Too many people lie around wishing for something different, or fantasizing about someone or something else instead of being present to the one who loves them. We give our partners a gift when we say specifically what we need and want, and join them in practicing the techniques.

All too often, rather than stating what we need and asking for it from another, we hide what we really want and then we resent the other person for not giving it to us. We assume the other knows what we want and refuses to give it.

I remember the most wonderful story from a collection about the wise men of Chelm. It told of a man named Mendel who wanted to borrow a sled from a friend, Goldberg. Before going to Goldberg, Mendel reviewed how he would he ask for the sled and assured himself that his friend would be glad to help him. Suddenly, because he was doing the transaction in his own head, it occurred to him that Goldberg might not lend him the sled. He was instantly affronted and upset.

He worked himself into such a dither about the fact that his friend was probably not going meet his need that he flew into a fury and stormed over to Goldberg's house in the middle of the night and pounded on the door. When the sleepy Goldberg came to the door, Mendel shouted in his face. He called him an ingrate for not wanting to lend him the sled and told him that he and his sled could go to hell. Goldberg was left bewildered in the doorway.

Mendel not only assumed his friend knew what he wanted, he assumed he was not going to give it to him. When **providing others with opportunities to give**, we must be explicit and then give them time to respond in their own way. We take responsibility for our needs by identifying them and asking. If what we need is not forthcoming in the way we need or want it, then it continues to be our responsibility to get the need met in some other way.

A key factor to keep in mind is that we have a large population from which to choose. If the person we ask cannot or will not give to us, we can ask others.

I have exasperated myself time and again by trying to get what I want and need from people who simply can't or won't give it to me. They don't even know how. This pursuit on my part goes beyond **providing others with the opportunity to give** to demanding that another be and do what I want. There is little joy in this. It almost never works. Meanwhile, others in my life would gladly give what I seek, but I ignore them in my insistence that it come in a particular shape and form and from a particular person.

I remember my years of cornering a close woman friend, demanding that she take interest in the consciousness studies I was pursuing. I wanted her to delight in them as I did, so that we would have something deep to share together. Alas, she was more drawn to how she looked, to horseback riding, and to the latest novel she was reading. The only area of consciousness that interested her was psychic phenomena. This bored me to tears. I continued to encourage, cajole, and pressure, but all to no avail. Many other friends would have made great companions in my exploration, but I was not as personally drawn to them. Instead, I persisted in trying to remake my friend to suit my needs. She never changed and I was perpetually unsatisfied.

Time and again I did this in my life. I longed to be loved and paid attention to by people who could not or would not meet my needs. I continued to focus on those very people. In the meantime, there were many in my life who were supporting, encouraging and loving me. Had I invested my time in them, my needs could have been filled.

Provide *many* others with the opportunity to give is the message here. And receive from as many as possible.

* * *

It is a risk to **provide others with opportunities to give**. It is a way of exposing self. When we ask of another, we reveal a need, a weakness, a limitation, and a desire. We reveal something of ourselves and we cannot know how the other will respond. This is the element of risk.

I used to know next to nothing about investing money. I said that I did not value it or care about it, but the truth was I had no idea how to proceed. I had a friend who was so terrific at investing that he did no other work. He had come into an inheritance and he learned everything he needed to know to make the money work for him. I knew that he could help me, but I did not relish revealing to him how little I knew about the subject. Nevertheless, I reached out to him.

Because I was self-employed, I was the one who had to provide my pension if I was to have one. I started a retirement plan, but I did it through my local bank and had my money tied up in certificates of deposit at a time when the interest rates were very low. At those rates, I would owe myself money by the time I retired. I had to do something, even if I had to expose my limitations. I called my friend.

As a result of **providing him with the opportunity to give** to me, I grew in my knowledge about investing and my retirement account began to swell. Even more, I learned that it brought him joy to teach me. It validated him, and it gave him an added way to express his love for me. Great profits accrued on multiple levels.

I benefited from my friend's knowledge and experience because I moved past the blocked energy I held about revealing my inadequacy. Once having opened and shared of my limitations, I moved into a state of love. I had **received myself as beautiful** and as a result I was able to empower myself through knowledge and learning.

* * *

At one time or another in our lives, most of us provide something larger than ourselves with the opportunity to give to us. The process is known as prayer. We ask God, by whatever name, to meet our need. There is no limit to what we include in our prayers, from success in a business deal to the recovery of a dying child, from desire for a mate to protection for a soldier, from the wish to win a contest to the hope for peace.

We reach to something larger as if there is a being in a heavenly office that we can mentally fax and have our request be granted.

It is important when we pray, even more important than when appealing to humans, to ask God with no expectations of being met or even of being heard. By this I mean we must learn to articulate truthfully what we seek and to **have no expectations** about how the prayer will be answered.

If we want success, our prayer should be about what we need to develop in ourselves to be successful. If we are praying about a dying child, we must consider that we do not know what is in the child's perfect life pattern and not be blinded by our own needs. If it is in harmony for the child to recover, so be it. If it is in greater harmony for this child to transcend this life form, it is not for us to demand the course of action that would most suit our desire.

When my father lay near death in intensive care in a Miami hospital, my mother prayed day and night that he would recover. He was unconscious and needed machinery to sustain his breathing and vital functions. My hopes for him were that he would not suffer greatly and when I prayed, I asked that the process he was experiencing would not be of long duration.

Then, I addressed my father directly. I spoke aloud to him, even though the doctors told me he was unable to hear. I told him that if he was ready to die, he could just let go and that we would release him. If he was not ready, I urged him to return to consciousness. I told him that he couldn't accomplish anything in this state. If he could bring himself back, we could at least communicate with him. I told him that my mother wanted a few last moments with him. She had things she wanted to say and I knew it would be important for him to hear them.

When I left him for the night, I insisted that he choose one direction or the other. Then I prayed that we would all have the strength to deal with whatever transpired.

The next morning, my father had returned. His eyes were open and he was responding to each of us. My mother was able to conclude her business with my dad, and my siblings and I had the opportunity to communicate our love to him. He lived for another week before making his transition.

I had **provided my dad with the opportunity to give** us the gift of his presence one last time. I knew I had no control over the situation, that we were all tenderly handling the fragile threads of life. Prayer served to center me, to align me with my strength, to be ready for all eventualities. I could see that my very personal experience of going to the edge of life with a parent was much more than that. It was a universal journey that we make time and again with loved ones until we ourselves make it alone.

If we pray to find a mate, we would be wise to pray that we develop ourselves to become the person such a mate would desire so that we might draw the mate to us.

Prayer is a way of bringing ourselves into alignment with what we are seeking. In prayer, we need to ask to see the ways to grow and develop to better meet our circumstances. Prayer is an active form of evolution in that we seek to lift ourselves out of our current limitations.

* * *

One of my personal early objections to the principle of **providing others with opportunities to give** was the danger that it might lead to dependence on others. I was fiercely independent. I valued taking care of myself and being responsible for fulfilling my needs. I was ensconced in the "I'd rather do it myself" syndrome.

I discovered there was another influence at work here. It was non-trust of others. Why let them in on the process or the activity? They would not do it as well as I did it. They would not follow through. Their efforts would need to be duplicated, re-done. Non-trust is disbelief that anyone can match my efforts, involvement, or commitment. If I do something, I know it is not only done, it is done the way I want it done. If someone else does it, I can never be sure of the results.

This perspective is deeply ingrained. For example, my partner is someone I can depend on, someone I trust and highly value. Yet, I still find myself checking to make sure she has handled a letter that needs to be answered, and wanting to know how she answered it. I exhibit this behavior even though we have worked together for nearly three decades. What is this about? It is about non-trust and it is about control.

When we are able to welcome others' efforts fully, we don't need to follow up on their actions. Instead, we can expand ourselves to welcome the unique ways in which they will do the task at hand. This is truly **providing others with the opportunity to give.** We let go of our private world views of how something should be done and we expand to welcome how they do it. In this we are all enriched, and stretched to a different and unexpected perspective.

Executive directors who allow for this within their organizations take tremendous burdens off themselves and encourage creativity and productivity. If a director needs to have a finger on everything that transpires, inefficiency reigns. In addition, many of the best and most innovative people will leave. They cannot thrive under restrictions that hold them bound in a singular perspective.

* * *

When the **Love Principle provide others with the opportunities to give** is applied to people we know, we open ourselves to be stretched, challenged, disappointed, amused, and enriched. We put ourselves on the line by voicing our requests and waiting to see what, if anything, will come.

Another whole range of discoveries comes from providing strangers with the opportunity to give. In the first place, we remove ourselves from communal separatism. Crowds of us can be in astonishingly close proximity and yet withdraw from each other to such an extent that there is no contact, no acknowledgment of the presence of others, no relating, and no relationship. It happens in busy elevators, on the subway at rush hour, on the avenues where hundreds walk in clusters, on the streets where drivers sit in isolated vehicles, in supermarket lines. We are together and yet we ignore each other.

This non-relating perpetuates a we-they world. It renders us non-feeling and enables us to look away in times of need because what is occurring is not directly affecting us. Instead of interweaving with life, we disappear within self.

To know the deepest dimensions of love, we must come forth and purposefully establish contact with others. The way I envision it is that I am part of One Self, and so is every one else. When I look at another I see the One Self we share.

Establishing contact with others in that One Self can be done simply. If someone is driving a car alongside mine, I can purposely turn my head and look in his direction. I can make eye contact, smile warmly, and complete the transaction by focusing again on the road in front of me. An action such as this, especially if I am consciously communicating my intention to greet another member of the human race, will not be misinterpreted as flirtation. It will be received, and it may be met. Then both of us will move on from it because we have consciously completed the transaction. I make this gesture frequently.

What is to be gained from such a contact? Meeting and acknowledging another human being eye to eye and soul to soul is a way of moving across chasms to call our group attention to the fact that we are functioning together in a network of mutual impact. Though we don't know the specifics of what is emerging from our joint effort, through a practice such as this we come to know that we are not alone and the singular lives we are living are very much interrelated.

We all know this phenomenon during times of crisis. All lines of distinction and all barriers fall away. We rush to contribute what is needed without thoughts of our personal selves. We become interactive units of powerful expression. Our innate nature breaks through and we each become part of a functional whole. It is as if we are one grand immune system and when there is trouble we rush in to protect the whole from extinction.

The shortcoming is that we retreat when the crisis ends. We pull our heads in like turtles and disappear within our shells of separation.

What if we were to be present to each other with this depth of presence when all is going well? When we are not threatened? We would extend to each other as if we were all related. We would remove any blocks to communion with one another, giving and receiving not only in equal measure but also as easily as inhaling and exhaling. We would relate to each other in love.

I stand only 5 feet 3/4 of an inch tall. Reaching for items on the top shelves in grocery stores is a challenge. It is a perfect and repeated opportunity for me to seek help from strangers. I have never been ignored or rebuffed. Those I have asked have met me fully and eagerly. There is joy in their faces to be asked and to be able to assist. And there is joy in me as I receive from them. We will probably never see each other again but we are united in a kindness.

In crowded elevators I used to retreat as far into myself as possible. On the one hand, it was a way of seeming to make physical space for others around me. It was also a way of creating psychic space. When I did this, however, I was really saying to all around me, "Stay away. Leave me alone. I want nothing to do with you."

Another way to deal with close quarters is to expand rather than contract. In these last years, I consciously envision myself as filling the entire space of the elevator car. Now, everyone in the car is inside my energy field. Each time I breathe, silently providing them with the opportunity to give to me, I draw in energy from everyone there. On the exhale, I release their troubles and concerns. In doing that, I am, in energy terms, lessening their burdens. When the doors open and we all scatter in different directions, we are the One Self going forth in many forms to do the work of humanity.

When we make eye contact with passers-by, and we smile and look in, soul to soul, we may be the only direct human contact these individuals have all day. We may be their lifelines. Those individuals who are troubled and have been contemplating violence to self or others, having been met, contacted, given to and received from, might change thought or emotional processes for the better. "Someone cared enough to look at me, to see me. Someone cared." It is that simple, and it happens every day. It is incumbent upon us that we recognize the importance of such actions, for we have a responsibility to be consciously present to others.

I learned about the higher levels of loving, and about the magnitude of this principle, by being on the receiving end of it. Someone reached out to me from the midst of a crisis and his reaching made that day one of the most meaningful of my life.

He was more than 2,000 miles away, in a phone booth at a fast food restaurant. He was having an anxiety attack and could not act on his own behalf. He did not see how to continue where he was going. He was unable to return to his home. He wept. His sobs made him seem no older than an abandoned eight-year old.

When he called he was clearly asking me to be there with him in his desperation. He provided me with the opportunity to love him fully, to receive him, to be present to him. I felt privileged to be able to give to him. I offered my love and my skills. A precious human being had scaled the walls of his despair and stretched a hand to me. There was nothing in my life that was more important in those long minutes than being fully present to him. My entire world was reduced to the spot in my office where I stood beside the file cabinet with the phone receiver to my ear.

I was able to be of help to him and he was able to take steps that eventually turned his life completely around. All of that is wonderful, but it represents the results rather than the process. The process was one of love, one of union, one of merging, and that is the true result **of providing others with opportunities to give.**

I was provided with an opportunity, but in giving, I received equally, and in receiving, he gave equally. This exchange was an act of conscious love. The energies flowed unrestricted between us and enriched us both as we held each other in a union of heart.

* * *

To **provide others with opportunities to give** is to acknowledge that we are integrated in a larger whole. It is to merge with others in a union of heart. It is to invite the blessing of unconditional love to flow between two human beings, thereby strengthening the whole.

* * *

Exercises for Practice:

1. Choose those persons in your life to whom you are always giving. Think of ways they can give to you from their talents and uniqueness, and make it a point to ask them to give to you.

2. Invite someone to help you with a project you know you can do perfectly well by yourself. **Have no expectations** about how they will express or participate. Allow yourself to be surprised.

3. Establish eye contact with one stranger every day. Ask *at least* one stranger every day to help you. Ask for directions, or for assistance with finding something in a store. Get in the habit of **providing others with opportunities to give** to you, and practice receiving.

CREATE YOUR OWN REALITY CONSCIOUSLY

I grew up in a run-down area of Brooklyn, New York. My entire life took place in a ten-block square of cement and concrete. Trees were few and far between and everything about the place spoke of rough and tumble. I liked my neighborhood. It had everything I needed. It afforded me the opportunity to play stickball and punch ball in the streets and to use the sidewalks for games of skelly and hopscotch. We did not have gangs in those days, but we did have tough kids. I was one of them. That was too modest! I should confess that I was a ruling force on my street.

Everything I have said is a reality creation. Had I created a different reality I might have reported that I grew up deprived, in a hostile, harsh environment. I might have said I had no real place to play so I had to resort to the streets.

When I have told others about my neighborhood, they have felt sorry for me. Perhaps because I did not know any better, I never felt sorry for myself in those early days. Instead, I felt strengthened and stretched. I needed to be innovative and imaginative. I needed to learn how to contend with difficulties. All of this built character and I was glad for it.

Our experience is a result of our perspective.

When we **create the reality** that our life is enhanced by the circumstances in which we find ourselves, we consciously love ourselves. We receive what is transpiring as supportive, enlivening, enriching, and expanding. We open ourselves with an eagerness that makes our lives exciting and unpredictable. We function with power because we are ready for any eventuality and we choose how we will respond. Nothing can undermine us or squelch our enthusiasm. We come to each moment awake and determined. We are full of purpose and committed to being the highest and best we can be in that moment.

All day, everyday, we are busy creating a reality of one kind or another. The catch is we may not know we are doing it. We may instead think, "This is the way things are." We think this because we are not **creating the realities consciously**.

We enter a room and say, "It is too hot in here." We focus on the room, and because "it" is hot, then we are hot. The reality we bestowed upon the room is now the reality we experience. If we would acknowledge that we are really creating the reality, we would enter the room and say instead, "I am too hot." Having said that, we are in a position to do something about our discomfort. We might check to see if we have on inappropriate clothing. Perhaps we have just been exercising and burning energy. We might be riled up about something and therefore overheated. Once we acknowledge that we create the reality and that we can do something about it, we can also check the temperature in the room. We would especially want to do this if others in the room indicate that they are cool, or at least comfortable.

What is important is that we do not make blanket, general statements, but rather that we focus on the personal experience we are having because we are creating it.

Life is energy and each of us forms and shapes that energy. The very life experience we have is a result of the forms and shapes we give it.

If we do not know that this is true, we become perpetual victims at the mercy of circumstances. We have the sense that life is being served up to us as a specific dish and we must eat it whether we want to or not.

I watch people living this way all the time. They get a call from a telephone solicitor and feel obligated to buy what is being sold. Or, someone tells them they are ineffectual and they simply take the critic's word for it, questioning self rather than the one who berated them.

If we know that we are the ones who are creating the reality of our lives and everything in it, we become choice-makers in every moment instead of victims.

I, for example, am an optimist. It is practically impossible to dim my spirits. In the face of disappointment, I bounce back and immediately search for another avenue for moving forward. I do this consciously and purposely. I choose it as a way of life.

In contrast to this, I have met countless persons who, without being aware that they are doing it, preplan their own daily disasters. They know in advance that something is going to turn out poorly and they are going to be hurt. They do not see that they are creating this reality and thus helping to bring it into being. Therefore, they say it happened to them. They become cynical and bitter. Their lives are very sad stories.

When we look for the good, for the constructive, we function from heart center. We breathe and expand in ourselves so that we call on all of our abilities and potential to deal with the current moment. We meet life unconditionally, acknowledging that still more is required of us to bring us into harmony with the situation at hand. We practice conscious love of life, just as it is. We become increasingly powerful the more we practice living this way. Everything becomes an opportunity.

* * *

Reality is defined as what is real. Yet, is there such a thing as "real"? At best, reality is what seems to exist and it is something we can collectively agree upon. A chair is placed before us and we all see it as a chair and know that we can sit on it. It appears to be a solid object, but in actuality it is not. What we call a chair is really a mass of vibrating molecules of energy. We cannot see the movement or the energy. To compensate for this, we "fill in the blanks." In response to what we are registering in the energy world, we form an image of it. Seeing our own mental image of the energy, we continue to abstract by giving it a specific name, definition, and function. Then, we agree that before us is a solid chair.

If we look at a ceiling fan that is not running, we say that it has three distinct blades. They are solid and real. Everyone would agree. Turn on the fan to full speed and suddenly the blades disappear. We can see right through them as if nothing solid existed. The fan blades are like molecules of energy. When those molecules, or blades, are spinning we cannot see them. Yet they are real.

When we look at a fan, we create the reality that the blades are solid and can be identified by color, texture and shape, but they are really swirling masses of energy even when seeming to stand still.

If we ponder this long enough it can be very disconcerting. We pick up a pen and begin to question what we are holding in our hand. A solid pen is one thing, but if we acknowledge that we are writing with a whirling mass of energy, we might forget why we sat down with the tablet.

On the other hand, if we realize that this is true, that reality is whatever we say is real, we can have any reality we want at any time.

We do not create life, or the energy world, but we do create our experience of it, how we see it, and what responses we have to it.

The experience we create of life directly affects whether we are empowered or disempow-ered. If we feel inferior to another, we have created that as a reality and it affects every reaction we have and every action we take.

The way we experience love determines the nature of the relationships we have. If we say we are not worthy of being loved, then that is the image we hold of ourselves. It may have no truth whatsoever, but if that is our reality then that is what is real for us. We create images of a lesser self and we cannot receive or experience love.

If we create the reality that we deserve to be loved, we immediately empower ourselves. If those we have chosen as lover or friend are not attending to us, we will look elsewhere because we know that we are worthy of the best.

We are the designers of the shape of our lives.

* * *

Everything simply is. That is, until we apply our preferences.

Several friends recommended a book to me. I could barely stand going through it. It was poorly written and simplistic. That in itself was a reality creation of mine. I have a set of standards and this book did not meet them. But I had gone beyond assessing the book to being disturbed about it, another reality creation of mine. The book was on the bestseller list. This was an affront to me.

In truth, the book was simply a book. All the other colorations from praise to disgust were reality creations.

The same is true of people. People simply are. They are alternately every expression of human nature, and they are capable of all things. We don't always remember this when we are interacting with others. We zero in on certain characteristics in them and use those to determine who we say they are. Whenever we think of them we think of these specific qualities and hold them bound in our view. But just because we hold them and see them in the ways we do, this doesn't mean they are as we perceive them. Nor are they how others see them or even how they see themselves. They simply are, ever changing and emerging.

When I was ten, I knew a boy whom everyone dismissed as a rotten kid. I had no doubt that he was. He always did and said mean things, and got into serious trouble. Richie was just plain bad and every one I knew held the same opinion.

Yet, in the midst of my labeling of him, I began to notice an opening in my perspective. There were certain things about him that appealed to me. He was wild and untamed. He was tough and sure of himself. He was not afraid of anything. He didn't care what anyone thought of him.

I secretly admired those qualities and found that they interfered with the general reality about Richie. Whenever I allowed myself to think of his free spirit, I couldn't see him as an evil kid.

Richie had a best friend, Eileen. She was as bad as he was. Together, they terrorized our city block. One afternoon, I was in my secret hiding place in the back alley and I heard the two of them talking quietly a short distance away. She was relating a problem she was having at home and he was responding with kindness and compassion. I could not believe it. I had never heard or seen either of them reveal this side of themselves. Neither fit the reality everyone held of them.

This was one of my first experiences of realizing that people are not necessarily what they seem. I also realized that someone loves even the most despised people and they also are capable of loving in the midst of their hating.

At the age of ten I did not quite know what to do with that experience. Today, as I am reminded of it, I see that both Richie and Eileen simply were who they were being in each moment. No matter what any of us decided about them, and in this case it was an entire neighborhood that held negative views, they were in no way locked into the reality we had created about them.

If we are not **creating our reality consciously**, we are being swept away by our preferences or by the general opinions others hold. Children usually function unconsciously by virtue of their undeveloped state. There is always one child who is singled out as a scapegoat. All the other children, without ever personally considering the matter, banish the outcast and make him the object of their ridicule. Occasionally one child in the midst of all the others begins to question the unconscious group choice. She looks afresh, uninfluenced by mass opinion. She begins to talk with the outcast and discovers him to be okay. She becomes his friend. She has created her own reality and done it very consciously. As for the larger group, they might be swayed from their thinking by her action. Their change of heart, however, would be no more conscious than was their rejection.

For the mass to **consciously create a new reality** about the banished boy, each would have to discover the boy for who he is.

In the fifth grade, a boy named Stanley sat in the last seat of the first row. He frightened my classmates and me because whenever he picked up a pencil his hand shook terribly and he was unable to write. He also spoke English with an accent and he held his head down most of the time, never looking into anyone's face. It was easy for the class to create the reality that Stanley was weird.

Our teacher was especially kind to him, but that did not transfer over to us. This was true even after we were told that Stanley had grown up in London during the Second World War and spent most of his early childhood taking cover to avoid the heavy bombing that was going on all around him. We were not any more sympathetic because we had no way to conceptualize war or living in a scene where bombs were dropped constantly. We simply could not understand; therefore, collectively, we stayed away from Stanley. We were ordinary, average kids who all behaved in similar ways and our preference was for Stanley to do the same. If he had to overcome some hardship that had occurred in his life, we wanted him to do it and get it over with so that he could fit into the accepted reality.

* * *

In addition to preferences, the meaning and value we attribute to events greatly colors the reality we create. To begin with, the event, any event, simply is. The most productive way to talk about it would be to make a non-loaded statement of description. For example, I remember the story of a woman in the Midwest who responded to an inner urge and moved from her chair seconds before the ceiling collapsed above where she had been sitting.

Our response to this statement will depend on the meaning and values we overlay on the event. We might say that she was lucky, or that her action was a fluke, or that she escaped her destiny and it will catch up with her another time. We might say that she was guided, or that she was saved. We might even value asking the woman herself for her response. But all of these evaluations are reality creations, which embellish the simple event.

If the woman involved was not **creating her reality consciously,** she was being moved rather than choosing to move. She would discover, after the fact, that she was no longer sitting in the chair. She would not know why she moved. On the other hand, if she were **creating her reality consciously**, she would be focused on the single most important moment in the event when she heard or felt an urging. She took responsibility for being present and for acting in relation to the urging. After the collapse of the ceiling, she would not only be grateful to be alive, she would be cognizant of a skill she had developed. She had taken action, without hesitation, in relation to an inner direction. She was developing her intuition. She was being obedient to what she was registering. She was attentive to the whole dynamic rather than just her need to sit in the chair. Her spiritual perception was greatly expanded. Knowing this would enable her to function more powerfully in all subsequent events because she had had verification that listening to the voice within was very wise.

Listening to an inner voice and paying heed required living in unblocked life energy, in love. The woman heard the voice and responded immediately. She did not put up objection or blockage. For example, she did not engage in a mental discussion in which she questioned whether she should or why she should move. She responded in love and consciousness, and the power of that saved her life.

* * *

More often than not, our realities are created in our private worlds. The private world is much like a filter system. We bring things into our awareness, run it through the filter of our private worlds, and what emerges is our interpretation of what came in and through. We hear what we hear, not necessarily what was said because what was said was filtered. We jump to understandings that may have little or nothing to do with what was being communicated. The filter system of the private world colors whatever we process.

An example of this is when a friend speaks strongly about an issue. That is the simple fact. If we receive the communication through our private worlds, we might say that our friend is angry with us. We would come to this conclusion if we have built into our private world filter the judgment that anything offered with strength is really anger.

In our private worlds we make all manner of assumptions about what is transpiring with another, about what something means, about what is being asked of us. Yet, the only way we can know if any of this is true is to ask. We will find very often that our interpretations are incorrect.

A way to break free of our private world domination is to be aware that the private world exists. Then, we can remind ourselves that we are jumping to a conclusion or that we are assigning meaning. Then we can ask the other and ourselves if our assessment is actually true.

Another way to move beyond the private world is to practice receiving each life experience in at least three different ways at once. If my partner tells me to go away for a while and my first private world response is that I have been rejected, I will immediately add two additional interpretations. A second response on my part might be, my partner trusts me enough to state his needs clearly. A third response might be, my partner is asking me for a gift and it is one that I can easily give.

When we practice this way, we stretch the confines of our filter system, and we constantly remind ourselves that we create our own reality.

After practicing three different ways of receiving, I might then, from a much more open place in myself, tell my partner I will honor the request and that I am also available should he want or need to talk.

The most important factor here is that I am not caught in any one way of viewing the transaction because that limits and disempowers me. The more open I am to possibilities, the more loving I am and the greater is my bank of choices.

* * *

Creating your own reality consciously usually begins with individualizing out of the groups with which we have been associated. This is often not easy. It could mean breaking with traditions, with long-held beliefs, with accepted ways of behaving. Our family and friends might be aghast at our new choices. These might range from insignificant to serious, such as deciding to wear raggedy clothes rather than dressing with "decency," or supporting a woman's right to choose abortion rather than seeing it as our mission to save life under any circumstance.

My sister and I hold different values. For example, my sister chose to move to Florida to be closer to our parents. This was never a value of mine. As my mother approached 90 years of age, she had a mild heart attack and subsequently, during her recovery, was sideswiped by a bus. My sister could not understand why I did not go to see my mother following those events. From her point of view, if my mother were to die without my seeing her again, I should feel guilty.

My point of view was altogether different. My mother and I talked at length several times about whether or not I should go to see her. We agreed that it was not necessary, and that talking on the phone a couple of times of week would serve just as well. I felt no unfinished business with my mother and, while I hoped I would see her many more times, I knew I would not feel guilty were she to die before I did see her again. I felt we were completely up to date, and I valued that even more than a visit.

My sister and I approach life differently. It is not that one of us is right and the other wrong. It is rather that we choose different values and live by them.

Values are arbitrary, even though many groups of people would have us believe that there is a definite right and wrong way of doing things. In my parents' generation, divorce was practically unheard of. Today it is commonplace and can be obtained simply because of irreconcilable differences. In my parents' generation, it would seem that convention was valued more highly than individuals and their needs. A person's fulfillment was less respected than keeping up appearances and not breaking commitments.

When we are still unconsciously identified with groups, it is often difficult for us to come to know who we are, what we hold dear, and what is vital to our evolution. The more imposing the group, the less chance there is for members to **create their own realities consciously**. There are groups that worship the "devil" and participate in rituals of sacrifice. The members are said to be brainwashed. But there are other groups that worship "God" who also brainwash their members and hold them bound in frightening belief systems in which they are threatened with hell and damnation. Their self-esteem is broken down because they are told they were born in sin.

There are groups that demand a food-fast one day a year in order that members be forgiven for their sins and have their name inscribed in the book of life for another year, and other groups that will absolve people every time they confess.

For most of our lives we are identified with groups. When we are functioning unconsciously, we tend to create the same realities the groups create. If the group is a race of people and that race holds stereotypes about other races, we, in our identification with the group, unconsciously hold and perpetuate the same stereotypes and the prejudices that result from them.

When we awaken to know ourselves as individuals, we can step back from the various groups to which we belong and evaluate the positions the groups hold. We can assess, from the broader perspective afforded us at a distance, whether we want to support the realities the group is creating.

When we choose to reenter those same groups or to enter new ones, as conscious individuals we will be in a strong position to choose the realities that are appropriate for us, no matter what the group is advocating.

As we grow in consciousness and advance along the path of individualization, we shift our allegiances. We choose to be in the company of people who reflect what we have come to know. The more we come to know, the more we change our affiliations. We choose groups that represent finer frequencies as we unfold into greater consciousness and take responsibility for the realities we create.

* * *

To **create realities consciously**, we must always question authorities and, in addition, question ourselves about our habitual ways of responding, which are mindless and unexamined. Habits can become so much a way of life that we rarely make a new choice about anything. Our routines are set and we embody them. The actions might have no life in them, no significance for us, yet we are so used to doing them that we sleepwalk our way through each day.

When we live by habit it is easy to become disgruntled by a change in our routine. The change causes us to act consciously, and if we are unaccustomed to functioning this way, it feels like hard work. Usually, we scramble to put things back in their place so that we can feel comfortable and our life is once again familiar and safe. The trouble with this is that life does not stay this way. It is full of surprises. It is not the same every day. It is changing all around us. Even if we are standing still, the very ground we stand on is moving. We can fight change only just so long before it knocks us off the illusory balance we were maintaining and sweeps us into what is emerging.

Very often people who enjoy standing still have their equilibrium disturbed when their company folds and they are left not only without their familiar habits but also without a job, income, security, meaning, and a predictable future. Or, their mate decides to leave, or dies. Suddenly their life is thrown into upheaval and coping is next to impossible because of the lack of practice in flowing with changes.

This is not to say that we can't have routines to depend on. We can. However, it is essential that we create the reality of those routines afresh every day. If we do that, we will **create our reality consciously** and we will enjoy what feels good and safe to us. Because we will be creating it each day, we will be aware that we can make new choices and that we are the creative beings who bring this reality to fruition. To know this is to be empowered.

* * *

There are two significant stages involved in training self to become adept at this **Love Principle**. The first is becoming conscious that we do create our reality, and that we do it continuously. In this first step, we begin to look at the kinds of realities we are and have been creating.

For example, I spent most of my childhood in fear. I constantly had the feeling that I was in danger. I developed a tough exterior as a disguise to ward off harm. I did not know why I felt so much fear, nor did I question it. It was "the way things were."

Years later, when I began to examine the fear with the objective of creating a new reality, I realized how often my mother exposed me to fear. She lived in constant worry and projected the worst scenario onto every experience. It was no wonder that I had developed a fearful response to life. I had done it unconsciously and it had become a habit.

In order to break the habit and create a new approach, I began to observe myself to see under what circumstance fear "jumped in" as an automatic response. After pinpointing trigger situations, I could more easily prepare myself for a new choice when the next similar circumstance arose.

It is important for us to be aware every time we say something "happened" to us. We must challenge ourselves to change that language and to begin to take responsibility for what we allowed to come into being without making a choice.

In the second stage, we learn to actually **create our own reality consciously**. We come to recognize that we were responsible for creating every old reality we ever held. It did not just happen and it was not the only way. We created it. Because we did, we can acknowledge that we have the power to undo it, to redo it, to do it differently.

With consistent practice, consciousness, deep breathing, and commitment to change, I gained creative jurisdiction over the fear I had been creating. I used to say that something or someone made me afraid. I came to know that I was the one who had been conjuring up fear unconsciously.

Once we claim this ability, we are ready to decide what reality we want to create in any life moment. We will especially want to practice this in familiar situations where it will be all too easy to tumble into a prefabricated response.

One of the big traps I have discovered in relation to this principle is the pitfall of non-acknowledgment. I have created a reality, even consciously, yet I do not want to admit that I have. If I admit it, then I must own up to my responsibility to change it. Sometimes, even if the reality I have created is unhealthy for me, I do not want to change it. If I do not acknowledge that I created the reality in the first place, I do not have to deal with my choice to continue to hold onto it, nor must I be accountable for changing it.

When I have fallen into this trap, I *think* I am functioning consciously. In truth, I have allowed myself to be ruled by my objective mind and its thoughts, judgments, and "shoulds." If I check my heart center I will find it is shut down. I am not functioning consciously, or with love, or with power.

I am most often entrapped in this fashion when another has spurned me in relationship. I dig my heels in and bring up a full measure of resistance. Then, rather than admit the resistance or that I have created a reality of separation and negativity, I speak badly of the other. I summon righteous indignation. I am the injured party and I remain aloof to my own embodiment of resistance. If I can get away with it, I will never admit that I am harboring any ill feeling. I speak only of how undependable the other is, and how unworthy of my attention.

This is a tough bind from which to release myself. I am so "right" about everything I feel and how I am choosing to express it, vile as it may be, that I am blind to the awareness that I am the one who is creating this reality. I do not want to know that I am. I don't want to be talked out of it. I don't want to change it. The aggravation is pleasing to me. Like a stirring volcano, I spew my heated temper in small bursts of condemnation.

It usually takes another conscious person whose heart center is open, to call me to consciousness under such circumstances. The friend might say, "Are you aware that you are creating a distasteful reality?" My immediate response is likely to be a spurt of hot lava in the form of an indignant "No!" But once my consciousness has been penetrated, it becomes difficult for me to sustain the antipathy. It feels so much better to be functioning in an open flow of life energy that I will be likely to release the feelings I have harbored and begin to create a new reality in which I at least move on and let go.

When I can admit to myself that what I am doing is lesser than my capability, I begin to move toward embodying my capacity. I begin to return to conscious loving and to great power of functioning.

The phenomenon I have just described is not only true of individuals; it is also true of interactions between nations. National policies are forged; actions against other nations are taken, and conflict or war results. However, the initiating nation refuses to take any responsibility for having created the reality. The leaders do not want it called to their attention and they seek to ignore the protests of even their own people. If they owned up to what they wrought they would have to take responsibility, admit errors, and bring about change. Such ego wounding is even more difficult for nations to handle that it is for individuals. If only the entire situation would simply fade away so that everyone could save face.

For nations to function with consciousness, they must *face* their mistakes, apologize, make new choices, and use the national energy to create new realities that benefit the whole world. If all nations were to cultivate this as a way of life, the energy of humanity would be focused on the creation of a harmonious world community in which international transactions were for everyone's advantage.

* * *

There are many who seriously misinterpret the meaning of **creating your own reality consciously**. They attribute powers to themselves that they do not have. They see themselves as being able to bring into being anything that they choose. They visualize, hold the thought, and seek to manipulate occurrences so that what they desire becomes a reality. If it does, they are confirmed in their supposed powers. If it doesn't, they are quick to explain it away with the overused phrase, "It was probably not in harmony." In both responses, they remain in the seat of importance.

The greater truth about this principle is that we are an active part of an all-encompassing reality that is always coming into being and is ever changing. It is a reality greater than any individual, group, national, and international or even planetary reality. I sometimes like to envision this grand reality as if it were a "wave" occurring at a universe-size ballpark. The energy has no identifiable beginning or end. It sweeps round and round, affecting everything and everyone in its path. It lifts us up out of the seats of our personal realities and envelops us with inspiration. The all-encompassing reality is the frequency world in which our true Self exists.

Our most important contribution to each emerging moment is to be present to what is being asked of us. What is there to bring forth from our uniqueness to meet what is transpiring? When we do this consciously we enter a state of cooperation with the frequency world and begin to have a sense of our place in the larger whole.

Several years ago in Gainesville, Florida, a small boy attending one of our sessions with his parents asked how we could possibly **create our reality consciously** while simultaneously **having no expectations but rather abundant expectancy.** His parents sought to hush him, but we encouraged his exploration because he enabled us to address the true position any of us occupies in the whole. In relation to our "inner" experience we have the power to create any reality we wish. With regard to the "outer" world, we can hope, dream, plan, even plot, but we are never in charge of how the total reality plays itself out. We can have abundant expectancy, and then wait. We can consciously apply ourselves to bringing into being the reality we would like to have reign, and then we wait. No single person dominates the whole; nor does any species. Each of us contributes; all of us wait.

The true process of creating a reality involves the making of very conscious choices in both the inner and the outer. We participate rather than determining. There can be nothing greater than this knowing of our connection to the grand design in which we are only single stitches. Through it we are inspired to deeper knowledge of ourselves and greater excellence of expression. When we know these truths and function in accordance with them, we become empowered.

* * *

Exercises for Practice:

1. When someone says something to you, observe how you interpret what you are hearing, and how you choose to respond. Take a breath, and add at least two different interpretations, and two different ways to respond.

2. Change your habitual reality creations. Comb or brush your hair with your other hand. Reverse the order of the chores you do each morning. Watch a TV show you would ordinarily never watch. Eat dinner at breakfast time and breakfast at dinnertime. In each situation, notice your reactions to discover whether or not it is easy for you to create a new reality.

3. Prepare a list of fill-ins such as, a. I'm the kind of person who _____, b. I am happy when _____, c. It bothers me to think _____, d. I get tired when _____. Jot down your answers at the beginning of a week. During the ensuing days, see if your answers are pure habit or if they truly represent you. At week's end, answer the questions again to see what new realties you are creating.

BE THE CHANGE YOU WANT TO SEE HAPPEN
INSTEAD OF TRYING TO CHANGE ANYONE ELSE

Most of us wish that we could change someone we know. My husband needs to express more tenderness. My teacher talks too much. My best friend is too dependent on me. My wife needs cooking classes. My child will not follow my instructions. The list is endless. Most other people just don't do it right, whatever it is!

I often joke that the one error in creation was that we were put in charge of our own lives. We are so much better at fixing others, at telling them what to do, when to do it and how to do it. We quickly see what is wrong with them, what needs improvement. We see it much better than they do. We see fault in others and remedies for them much more easily than we see the same in self. If each of us was in charge of one other's life, all of us could create a perfect human race.

Alas, it does not work that way. We were given ourselves to manage, to observe, to improve, and to develop.

No matter how diligent we are about getting someone else to change, either they don't or they won't. Or if they do, the result is never quite what we had in mind. Even if they change to please us, the change usually does not last and they fall back into their habitual ways of functioning.

Trying to change another is a futile effort. In addition, it is not a very loving thing to do because we are saying that we will not receive the other as beautiful as he or she is. We are blocking our love flow in relation to other, holding back, and being conditional in our relating.

Ironically what we see in others that distresses us, often exists in ourselves to some degree. It is something we do not like in ourselves; therefore, we absolutely cannot stand it in someone else.

For example, there is a person in my life who can be mean, cruel, witch-like, battering, and downright ugly. If I could change her, I would do it in an instant. One of the great shocks of my life was when the person closest to me told me that I occasionally had "battering witch" tendencies in *my* nature. It was the last thing I wanted to know about myself. But knowing about it at least enabled me to do something about it. As long as I was unaware of it, "the witch" would simply come out and take over whenever I was not making conscious choices about the reality I wanted to create.

Once I was made aware of it, because of its impact on a loved one, I could listen for it. And, I could make a new choice when it was present. I am glad to say that it rarely manifests anymore because of all the work I have done in relation to it.

Therein lies the key to change. I wanted to do something about it. I wanted to change the behavior. One of the reasons it is so difficult to get others to change their ways is that before they can, they must want to. Once they do want to, and do change, the credit is all theirs. Even though I may have made the suggestion or the demand, if they wanted to and they changed, it is their accomplishment, not mine.

Be the change you want to see happen instead of trying to change anyone else. When I do this I am consciously loving because I open to something more in myself and allow it to become a reality. By embodying the quality I see missing in another, I bring that quality into the world. That is an act of conscious loving, by hopefully making the world, or at least the part of it I affect, a better place.

I am aware that I fill most days with opinions and complaints. I observe societal flaws, put down politicians, grumble about policies, despair about conditions of life. Every time I do this I want *someone else* to **be the change I want to see happen**. I want someone else to make sure everyone has health care. I want someone else to be honest and full of integrity. I want someone else to change a law or do away with poverty. What about me? I am the one who needs to be in myself what I would have others become.

Then a familiar voice rises up to excuse my inaction. I cannot **be the change I want to see happen** because I do not have the power. I am just an average citizen. How can I possibly affect society? I do not hold any office; I cannot make laws or determine policy. I cannot create health care, or eliminate hunger, or stop gang killings.

Whenever this voice speaks, I challenge it. I can do just about anything. All I need to do is begin. I can do what I can as who I am, and as I become more effective as who I am, I can do more. In acknowledging myself in this way, I consciously love who I am and what I have the potential to be. The more I do this, the more I empower myself, and the greater my actual accomplishments.

I mentioned at the beginning of this book that the **Love Principles** came into being as the result of **The Love Project** enacted at a ghetto high school in Brooklyn, New York in 1970. That, for me, was my first great example of **being the change I wanted to see happen**.

The time period was a difficult one in United States history. The nation was involved in an undeclared war in Vietnam, anti-war protests were at their height, disrespect of authority was rampant, and the neighborhood was in upheaval over New York City budget cuts that gravely affected services for the people. The slums around Thomas Jefferson High School were in a constant uproar of violence and firebombing. Student deaths to drugs and random gunshots were epidemic. Teaching was next to impossible because of absenteeism, student learning difficulties, and the need of students to focus on survival rather than education.

I was a teacher. I had little or no power. I was not in a position to impact society as a whole, nor was I a politician or a policy maker. I was not deciding curriculum. I was not a principal. I couldn't even get my students to look to any future, or to want to live, let alone to want to learn.

Others on the staff had given up on every level. And who could blame them? There was no hope. The one thing I had in my favor was that I had not given up. I hoped for and wanted change. I wanted the faculty to become enthusiastic, but I knew I could not change them. I wanted the students to come to class, to be attentive, and to learn. I knew I could not make them do it. I wanted the society to turn from war and commit to loving one another. I knew I had no way to turn that tide. I wanted death to pull up its black robe and reveal new birth that had a possibility of surviving in the midst of brokenness. I knew I had no power over death, or life, or brokenness.

I was David, and Goliath was too damn big.

Every place I looked outside myself, there was nothing I could do. But inside, inside the incorruptible core of me, I was all-powerful. I wanted change and I could be it. I wanted a new reality and I could create it. So I did.

I began as a single person and provided others with the opportunity to join me. I wanted there to be love, so I became love. With a handful of students and two other teachers at my side, I began by **being the change I wanted to see happen.** We turned the school and the community around in a period of seven months. A small band of ordinary folks, armed with the best of intentions and the power of commitment, brought learning, caring, and renewal to the pits of despair. We did not need anyone else to change. We were **being the change we wanted to happen** and because of that we could do anything, be anything, bring anything into being. And we did.

As a result of **The Love Project** the environment became conducive to learning, students looked forward with excitement to coming to school, reading improved, and human relations took a big turn for the better. Students developed self-esteem. They felt hope and a sense of purpose. They began to see that they could change their miserable circumstances. They found reasons to plan for the future. Previously, they did not know they had a future.

* * *

There is tremendous power in this **Love Principle**. It can lead to change in any area from personal interactions to international relations. Love is unblocked life energy and **being the change you want to see happen** enables the release of unlimited energy. It is important to remember as we embody what we want to see come into being, that it is imperative that we **have no expectations**. We can know what we want and we can go about creating it, but we must always hold in our consciousness that we are a small part of a large whole. What we seek and what we create are affected at every step of the way by the movement of the larger universe in which our desires and actions are occurring. As we impact that universe, so too are we impacted. Therefore, a good way to proceed in every aspect of life is to take a small step forward and, before taking another, observe what the small step has brought into being. Then, every step will be one of cooperation.

If we want a loved one to be more enthusiastic, we need to be more enthusiastic ourselves. We must find as many varied ways as we can to express delight and to be fervent. We must never do this with the intention of showing the loved one how he should be, or even with the hope that he will change as a result of experiencing our behavior. Such an intention on our part will usually lead to disappointment and will be very disempowering. We do not love him if we have an agenda for him and hidden expectations.

We should embody enthusiasm because it pleases us, because it is an expression we value, because it strengthens us, and because there is a dearth of it when we are with the loved one and we hunger for it. Even if the other does not notice or never changes, everything will have changed because we will have integrated enthusiasm. We will be more pleased. We will be strengthened. Our hunger will have been satisfied by our own action. Our need for the loved one to be enthusiastic will have decreased because our own expression of enthusiasm will have increased.

Being the change you want to see happen shifts the balance and changes any transaction from what we wanted it to become, to what we are now creating.

By being the change we can actually change the world. This is certainly a statement of power. Again, it is vital to proceed with no expectations, especially about how long it might take to change the world. It is always better to begin with what is in front of us, proceeding one step at a time, observing and cooperating as we advance with open heart centers and a conscious love flow. It is in this course of action that our power resides.

In 1970, as part of **The Love Project** at Thomas Jefferson High School, a great issue was raised about equality. Students were constantly being harassed about smoking in the school building. It was not permitted. Yet, teachers could smoke in their lounges and in their cafeteria.

The first alternative proposed was that the students also be assigned designated smoking areas. That would have brought about equality, which was the change being sought. However, having taken that one step forward, several dilemmas arose. Did we, as responsible educators, want to encourage students to smoke by providing them with a designated area? We did not. That "we," included the smokers among us. I was one of them.

The group involved in **The Love Project** proposed that we discourage all smoking by eliminating all smoking areas in the school. We were not very popular. I remind you that this was taking place in 1970 when the focus on the impact of tobacco on health was not nearly as great as it is today.

In the midst of the discussion about the dilemma, someone involved in **The Love Project** discovered that a New York City law stated that there might be no smoking at all in any public school building. Although teachers complained that as teachers they deserved more rights than students, the principal decided to ban all smoking.

A handful of us was **being the change we wanted to see happen** and suddenly a revolution began on many levels. Many of the teachers who smoked began to reduce the number of cigarettes they smoked each day because they had to go outside. Some of them gave it up altogether. One had an experience that affected her deeply. She was smoking outside the building and talking with one of her students who asked her for a cigarette. Since she was smoking she could hardly lecture the student on the ills of the practice. She gave up the habit within a week.

Some teachers were forced to look in the face of their addiction for the first time. That put the drug addictions of their students in a new light.

The smoking ban was accompanied by a school-wide campaign against smoking and the American Heart Association and the American Cancer Society cited Jefferson High School in their national communications as an example of the change that could occur. What we did at Thomas Jefferson was the beginning of a nation-wide campaign against smoking in schools, and it expanded into the elimination of smoking in air-planes, office buildings and public buildings.

This is what I mean by **being the change you want to see happen.** Take a step at a time, **have no expectations** about the results or how long they might take, and observe how what is relevant in one small unit, mushrooms when it is in harmony with what is emerging in the universal dimension. Any of us can, in truth, help change the world.

* * *

Being the change you want to see happen requires proper defining of terms. When I say what I want, it needs to be something I, by myself, can make happen.

I had a friend who was in an abusive relationship. The abuse went on for years until she couldn't stand it any longer and sought an end to the way she and her husband were living. She began by saying that the change she wanted was for him to stop beating on her. Phrased this way, she was not empowered because she was focused on changing her husband.

As time went on, she reassessed and rephrased. She identified the change she wanted to see happen as wanting her husband to be kind, gentle, loving, and supportive. This was a good beginning, but it was still focused on and what she wanted *him* to do. The change could happen only if he wanted what she wanted.

My friend needed to define and refine statement of what she wanted. She desired to be treated with kind-ness, gentleness, love and support. She needed first to do that for herself.

She needed to ask herself what actions would be

required on her part? What was the kindest thing she could do for herself? She considered counseling help. She thought of drawing boundaries around what she was willing to accept and not accept as a way of loving herself. Her greatest liberation came when she realized that the most supportive thing she could do for herself was to immediately leave the situation and put herself in an environment of safety.

If she had tried to convince herself that her husband would change, she would have been setting herself up for further abuse. She might even have encouraged her own eventual death at his hand. This would not have been an act of self-kindness.

Furthermore, if she had not changed toward herself in this relationship and become her own advocate, then even if she had left the marriage, she would likely have created a similar reality with someone else in the near future.

The learning for my friend and the relearning for me was the need to define terms and embody wishes. We must all make our lives what we want them to be without wasting another minute trying to get someone else to change his or her behavior so that we can be safe or happy.

* * *

Be the change you want to see happen enables us to become powerful initiators of new ideas and new ways of being. We are the ones who see the change that needs to happen and we are the ones who can make it happen. Living this principle requires ingenuity, application and commitment, but it does not necessarily require anything outside of ourselves. Whatever we see, we can be. We will be stretched in the process because we will need to change in order to make the new happen. But with **no expectations** of what will happen or how it will happen, we also leave ourselves open to be surprised by what we set in motion.

A very clear example of this dynamic happened for me in the early 1980's. From 1953 to 1971, I was a professional actor on Broadway, in commercials, in television and in film. I also directed and taught acting. One of the elements of the profession that left me dissatisfied was the lack of emphasis on the art itself. Although I loved performing, especially before a live audience, I loved creating the new role even more. I loved the deep work of bringing a character into being who existed only on paper and in the writer's mind.

In 1969 I experienced a breakthrough to cosmic consciousness and was changed forever in terms of how I knew myself and my relationship to the whole. As I moved toward new ways of being, and different expressions of my talents, I moved away from professional theater. However, my attraction to acting remained a burning ember at the core of self.

Eleven years later, after a move from New York to San Diego, a departure from my marriage, and the commencement of a spiritual work with Diane Kennedy Pike, the theater still called to me. I knew I did not want to return to New York, or to live in Los Angeles, or to return to the "cut throat" aspect of the profession.

I couldn't move creatively in myself because I did not know what I wanted. As I said earlier, this is key to being the change.

I continued to probe in my consciousness and in my desires. What emerged repeatedly was my focus on the art rather than the profession.

Then it came to me. I wanted to see the art combined with personal spiritual unfoldment. Ordinary persons could easily use the process an actor uses to create a role for the stage to create the life they are living. As the actor knows she is merely playing a role but is not that role, so too can conscious persons come to know themselves as the Player who brings the personality or character into being each day. Knowing this, and actually doing it, is profoundly empowering in that it enables people to have creative jurisdiction over the various components of the self.

This was the change I wanted to see happen not only in participants but also in my own application of my talents. I set about to be that change and brought **The Theatre of Life** into being in 1981. The program trains participants to know themselves as the Player who creates the character through which they enact their days on life's stage. Participants learn they are not their personalities and can therefore change who they appear to be at will. They are taught to create feelings rather than have them and therefore, be had by them. Working with the four main components of self, the participants work toward conscious alignment of the Self.

Since its inception, **The Theatre of Life** has enabled hundreds of participants to live more powerful and conscious lives.

The process involved in the creation of **The Theatre of Life** began with a dissatisfaction in me that caused me to move on from a profession. But there remained a stirring, a desire to participate in the art form. Once I moved past thinking I needed to return to my former career to satisfy the longing, I opened to what I actually wanted. What emerged went beyond any **ex-**

pectations I might have had. What I arrived at did not exist. No one had yet brought it into being. I could see it; therefore, it was for me to be it. I set it all in motion, designed the program, brought it into being, and offered it to those who were already working with us in our workshops. It has been in existence ever since and is serving people very profoundly in their awakening process.

* * *

I suspect that **be the change you want to see happen** is at the core of the evolutionary process. Every time one of us needs something greater to come into being and we become it in and through ourselves, we bring about an advance in human development. Think of it. Candlelight was inefficient. Someone said, "This needs to change," and so it did. It used to take a long time to cross continents by ground transportation. Someone said, "We need to fly," and the world changed forever.

In this sense, those things that distress or irritate us are stimulants to our creativity. They urge us on and force us to bring the new into being through ourselves. Each of us is equally blessed in this regard because any of us can **be the change we want to see happen** in any area of our lives. If we are not pleased with what we bring into being, we can try again, refining and honing until what we make manifest matches what we are seeking. The power resides in remaining open and allowing heart energy to flow. Change emerges from being in a state of love in which we respond unconditionally to life stimuli.

Knowing that we can always, and at any time, **be**

the change we want to see happen makes us very powerful human beings.

* * *

Exercises for Practice:

1. Choose a behavior in a loved one you wish would change. Embody that change yourself, fully and joyfully every day. **Have no expectations** that anything will change in your loved one. Instead, observe how *you* are changing and how your view of things around you is changing.

2. Choose an issue that stirs your passion. Make it one you wish others (politicians, authorities, etc.) would do something to change. **Become the change** you wish by starting in your own neighborhood and in your own circle of friends and family.

3. Every time you feel strongly about something, never stop with expressing an opinion. Always think of at least one action you can take and *do it.*

RECEIVE ALL PEOPLE AS BEAUTIFUL
EXACTLY AS THEY ARE

Receiving people as beautiful exactly as they are is no easy task for any of us who have opinions, judgments, and even feelings about how other people should be. And most of us do!

From our vantagepoint, we can see exactly what is wrong with another. Not only that, we know precisely what they need to do to shape up. While we say our focus is on improving them for their own good, our real purpose is to make them into who we want them to be because it would be easier for us to relate to them.

If we were as successful as we imagine we would be, we would eliminate diversity and make the rest of the human race, clones of ourselves.

What we would miss in such a process is who the others are and why they are the way they are. We would miss what drew us to the differences. We would miss what there was for us to learn. And, we would miss how we might stretch and grow as a result of receiving the challenge and stimulation.

Sometimes we wake up too late to what our opportunities are. My parents were married for 63 years. In their last years together when they were in their early 80's, my dad, after a lifetime of hard work, settled deeper into his retirement leisure. He watched television, read the paper, smoked cigars, and reclined by the pool at their condo. My mother, a highly energetic and intelligent woman who was also controlling and a master at worry, began confronting what had been missing in her life and marriage. She wanted an equal companion. Although my father was a good person, he had not filled my mother's needs. She took the occasion of those leisure years to nag my father. She compared him to other men, pointed up his shortcomings, and tried to shame him into changing. She also engaged in shouting matches with him. There were times when the two of them argued so fiercely that I threatened never to come to visit them again.

I encouraged my mother to get out into the world and give herself what she needed by way of intellectual stimulation and meaning, but she continued to want my father to become the image she held in her head. She did not **receive him as beautiful** as he was and insisted that he change.

Relations between them worsened. They were caught in a destructive cycle and they did not know how to extricate themselves even though their three children tried everything we knew to help.

Eventually my father's health deteriorated. He couldn't stand the dynamic anymore, and his legs literally gave out beneath him. During the months of his decline, including long hospital stays, my mother was always at his side. She poured her energy into concern.

After my father died, my mother's grief was overwhelming and long lasting. She missed him terribly, even though he had not been the companion she had needed. The focus as she talked of him after his death was not so much on his shortcomings as on how much she had loved him. While he was alive she had someone to talk with, or at least to talk to. Her complaints turned to regrets.

One of the main reasons we do not **receive others as beautiful as they are** is that the lacks we see in them often represent opportunities for our own growth. Had my mother received my father as beautiful as he was, she might have learned something from him about relaxing, about not needing to function at a constant frenetic pace. She might have found a more creative outlet for her own vitality and energy. She might have acknowledged who she was and what she had to offer. Instead of berating him for having no interests and for doing nothing, she might have been listening to what she was actually saying to herself: "I am not involved enough in activities to keep pace with the substance of myself. I am not doing anything important with my life." She might have **become the change she wanted to see happen** in him.

Whenever we do not receive another, we miss an opportunity. In their last years together, my mother and father did not **receive each other as they were**. In that, they missed a great opportunity.

* * *

Of all the **Love Principles**, the most powerful, liberating, and difficult is **receive all people as beautiful exactly as they are.**

Over the years, since the inception of the principles in 1970, people have sought to reword this one more than any other. Most especially there has been resistance to the word "beautiful." Those with objections proclaim that everyone is not beautiful, that there are horrible people who do horrible things and that they should be condemned rather than received. The only way objectors have been able to get around the issue is to separate perpetrators from their actions: "We can love the persons but not what they do."

This approach not only separates the persons from their deeds, but it fails to grasp the true meaning of the principle. Instead of activating the power that comes with conscious loving, such an approach leads to rationalization and supports a weakened love expression that is by no means the unconditional love the principle represents.

In order to embody this principle, it is necessary to function from the heart center rather than the mind. The first word is "receive," as differentiated from "accept." To accept people suggests the use of mental judgment. Based on our opinions and private world views, we assess whether or not people are acceptable. If they are, it is because we agree with them at least to some extent. Acceptance is loving based on preference or approval.

To "receive" means to open, to let in, and to be present to, without opinion or thought, and also without activating preferential feelings. Therefore, neither the mind nor the solar plexus is activated with this principle. At work is pure heart center energy. This is not familiar or easy for most individuals.

To receive means to welcome, and to **have no expectations** about who or what will come but to be prepared to meet everything equally. The focus is more on our own state of being, on our preparation.

A perfect example is Mahatma Gandhi on the day of his death. He was warned not to go out into the crowd at the Prayer Meeting to greet people because his life had been threatened. However, his focus was on **being the change he wanted to see** in the world. He did not proceed with fear or hesitation. When the moment came, he met and received his assassin face to face. As he was shot, he maintained his openhearted demeanor, receiving this act as part of the perfection of his whole life. Without ever skipping a beat, he bowed to his assassin and pronounced the name of God (Ram) as the bullet struck him. It was his final uttered word.

Gandhi's focus was not on labeling the behavior of the man who took his life. It was rather on what he was doing and being. He received the moment of his death, and the person who brought him to that moment, as beautiful, just as he received all other moments.

To "receive all people" means exactly what it says. It means everyone, no matter who they are, how they express themselves, what they do, or how they look. It means that every person is recognized as having equal value in the big picture of things. It is an acknowledgment of the wisdom that we are all individual expressions of One Greater Whole.

We do not practice this principle if we love some people and not others. To the degree that we withhold energy from some persons, to that extent do we also withhold energy from those we actually love. When we hold back, we withdraw a part of ourselves and that part of self is not accessible to us. We cut ourselves off from the fullness of the love current when we inhibit the flow in relation to selected people. Any diminishment of the stream is a lessening of the power in us. In short, we cannot have it both ways. We cannot be infused with limitless vitality and then offer it to others conditionally. What we give is what we bring to ourselves.

Loving consciously means loving more than the select few with whom we have an affinity. We love only certain people when the love comes from the solar plexus rather than the heart center in which we touch unconditional love. Through the solar plexus, the feeling component of self, we are personally drawn to another. We want to be with the other, to give and to get. We can easily be exhilarated or hurt by what the other does or says. We are in love.

Solar plexus love is reserved for special people in our lives. We do not fall in love with everyone. However, the nature of solar plexus love is that as easily as we fall in love, so too do we fall out of love.

When we love from the heart center, we love the person without any specific reason. We do not have a personal attachment or need. We love because we are committed to loving. Therefore, the person before us is there to be loved.

I try to imagine sometimes what the world would be like if everyone functioned this way. No matter where we would go or whom we would meet, we would love and be loved. We would be safe, protected, cared for. Everyone else would feel the same in our presence; remarkably, in everyone's presence.

And why shouldn't it be this way? We are all expressions of the same One Being. It is profoundly unhealthy for us to dislike, withhold from, or hate another part of our One Self. It is like having your shoulder send a stream of negative feelings toward your thumb. What an incredibly non-productive thing to do!

Receive all people! We cannot know the extraordinary joy and sense of union that derives from this practice unless we are willing to embody it. The resultant joy is accessible all day, everywhere.

So many times, while waiting in an airport, I will connect with people around me, eye to eye and heart to heart. Their faces immediately soften and warmth emanates from them. Words are not exchanged; love is exchanged. I receive them and the power of that cuts through our status as strangers. After doing this everywhere and being surrounded by soul to soul exchanges, the truth of Oneness is palpable to me. I know I am a member of the family of humanity and I feel related to everyone I touch (and even to those I do not).

Receive all people "as beautiful." I consciously create the reality that all humans are beings of equal intrinsic worth. Each plays a unique role. Each has special attributes. Some of us make a more visible contribution than others, but all of us make contributions to the unfolding whole. Each contribution, large or small, is equally important in the total picture.

When I sit down to eat a salad, I almost always see an image of stooping farm workers. They are most often persons from other countries who work for minuscule wages during long hours in the hot sun. Without them, the wealthy landowner would have little benefit from his or her crops, and the rest of us would not have fresh green food to enjoy. The owner, the foreman, the farm worker, the truckers, the market managers, the checkout clerk, and the consumer, all play equal roles in the total dynamic. When I sit eating my salad, I offer gratitude for all who made it possible. This practice reminds me to hold all people everywhere in equal respect and love. We are all part of a larger cooperative that enables creative growth and change to occur in every moment.

As I reflect on this theme, I touch into a sense of God, in whose image we are all created, as the total body in which each of us is a cell. Stated simply, I see all living things as the God-force itself, embodied.

What this means to me is that all is of God, both spectacular waterfalls and disastrous floods, benign and poisonous snakes, cactus flowers and marijuana. I know the same is true of human beings of every race, color and creed, healthy or diseased, criminal or saint, aged or infant, homosexual or asexual, conservative or socialist. All are of God. All are in the world as a part of the whole. I am one with them as they are with me. What happens to any one of them affects me and everyone else, even if I am unaware that this is true.

All people are beautiful to me because they are matchless pieces of the whole. They are expressions of life's diversity.

I was raised with concepts of right and wrong, acceptable and unacceptable, and it caused me to separate people and events into good and bad categories. It did not take me long to realize that the categories were merely arbitrary. The negative feelings I held toward one set of people, a third set of people held toward me. It was clear that every group could be stereotyped, diminished, or exalted. It was all reality creation.

During my spiritual breakthroughs, I touched deep within myself my inseparable connection with all that is. I came to know Oneness, namely, that there is one creative force that I choose to call God. If there are such things as the devil or evil, they too are of God.

What has been reduced to good and evil, to God and the Devil, I came to know as the polarities of the creative force. These polarities are the yin, or manifesting force, and the yang, or initiating force. They are in a constant, dynamic, creative interaction with each other for the larger purpose of allowing life to evolve.

As I am constantly growing and evolving, I know that this is also true of everything and everyone. Because we are cells in the body of God, clearly God is also constantly evolving.

I had always thought of perfection as a "finished" state and of God as perfection. I now see that perfection has an ongoing dimension to it. There is no end to perfection's unfolding. While perfection means complete in every respect, complete has evolution as one of its components.

Anything that is complete in the sense of fixed eternally would certainly be dead.

The natural world, and all life in it, is constantly changing. Human capacity has expanded remarkably since our first emergence. In just the last one hundred years we have harnessed electricity, developed motorized vehicles, learned to fly, traveled to outer space, established instant communication, created television, broken every sports record, and on and on.

My sense of God, of the God-force, of the Creative Principle is of an evolving, changing, expanding, living, and dynamic process.

I am wary of any belief system or philosophy that is rigid, fixed, immovable, dead. I know that such a belief system is perfect and I receive its promoters as beautiful exactly as they are. They are playing their role in the grand design. However, for my own well-being and unfolding, I do not affiliate myself with any group that proclaims that its doctrines are the unchanging truth, and that their way is the only way to function. Dogmatism and rigidity do not lead me to growth. To say there is only one way is really to say "I am unwilling to see anything else because I have locked myself into this singular belief system." As a highly complex being in a highly complex world, I want to stay open to the full range of possibilities in every moment. I am in relationship with all that is around me. All that is, is of the One Self.

Speaking of the One Self, to say or to believe there is only one way to do things would be like having a stomach cell proclaim to the cells of the brain that salvation is to be found in digestion and therefore all brain cells must convert and become stomach cells. If the brain cells all converted, they would quickly render the body dysfunctional.

Evil is described not only as bad, but also as causing pain, as harmful, as bringing misfortune. By this definition, the grandest form of evil would be Nature herself. Through earthquakes, tornadoes, floods, and fires, Nature causes havoc, is harmful, and brings unspeakable pain.

We have made peace with the "evil" of natural forces because we know that we have no control over them. We don't always like the results. We wish Nature would not destroy. But we know that the conditions of our planet are something with which we have to live. Those same conditions grant us life in the first place. We know that Nature's disruptions are part of a larger harmony that is beyond our understanding.

The same is true of the entire behavior and action of human beings. Every expression is part of a larger whole that none of us from our vantage point as single cells can possibly come to know. Everything has its place and is part of the expanding, evolving perfection.

On a drive around Lake Tahoe in Northern California many years ago, I marveled at the beauty of the huge, round boulders that rested on the sides of mountain slopes. I suddenly pictured myself there, in that spot, millions of years ago when the earth was in fierce turbulence and these boulders were being flung through the air. Had I been alive then I might not have appreciated Nature's exhibition of power. But from that day's vantagepoint, when the earth was at rest and the mountains were holding their shape, I was in awe rather than terror. I saw beauty, not evil.

A similar perspective is needed with regard to the actions of human beings. How can anyone receive Hitler as beautiful, as part of a larger perfection? Or anyone who helped to run his death machine? An overview of history from the vantage point of a half-century later allows me to see that his profound ability to harness power required the allied forces of the rest of the world to join together in a common effort to stop his onslaught. Perhaps one of Hitler's roles, as a cell in the body of God, unknown even to himself, was to encourage joint cooperation and to teach evolving cells how to live together and support one another in a common purpose. His actions brought the United States out of isolation and forced us to accept our responsibility in the world community.

The common effort referred to here was all-out war in which the allied forces sought to wipe out the enemy. For this effort to be an act of conscious love, all the principles would have had to function together as one whole. The heart centers of the allies would have had to be open enough to **receive** Hitler **as beautiful** in playing his part while they were simultaneously **being the change they wanted to see happen** by seeking with all their might to stop his appalling actions. If they had determined that **their opportunity, in the problem** he was generating, was to stamp out the horror he was perpetrating, then they would have galvanized all their power to **create a new reality** throughout Europe.

The point is, we can **receive someone as beautiful exactly as they are** and, at the same time, take the action we deem necessary in order to **consciously create the reality** we want to bring into being. It is not necessary to hate another, or even to call him evil. Each of us must pursue what there is for us to be and do.

Having been born into the Jewish heritage, **receiving** Hitler **as beautiful** was a particularly hard challenge for me. Yet, had it not been for Hitler, I suspect there never would have been a State of Israel. His actions so impacted the conscience of the world that a homeland for Jews was allowed to become a reality. Hitler played a major role in that. It is probably the one thing for which he would never want credit.

How could anyone receive the Holocaust as beautiful exactly as it was? Some, who suffered the Holocaust and survived, discovered the importance of meaning. As a result, their lives were changed for the better forever. Others were imprinted with a greater awareness of responsibility in relation to fellow human beings. Others vowed that they would be the conscience of humanity, guaranteeing that we would never forget the horror of the Holocaust and never let it happen again. These persons represent vital growth in the unfolding of human consciousness, and a man most associated with evil evoked that growth. Would we have preferred that growth to come in another way and without the sacrifice of millions of lives? Of course. But nevertheless we can rejoice in the growth that came.

Betsie ten Boom, who died in an extermination camp, was an example of someone who knew of the perfection of all things. Her spiritual focus was on Jesus. Through him, she learned to give thanks for everything, no matter what the circumstances.

She and her sister Corrie were arrested for hiding Jews in their home. When they were herded into the camp in a frightening assault on human dignity, Betsie expressed gratitude for the "jammed, crammed, stuffed, packed, suffocating crowds" because she was able to slip past the guards without having to give up her Bible.

Later, during their horrendous incarceration, Betsie gave thanks for the dreadful fleas and lice because the inmates had greater freedom in their quarters. The guards did not want to subject themselves to the critters. Her focus was never on her hardship, but rather on showing others that in all cases "love is greater" than any vicissitude.

Betsie ten Boom had consciousness great enough to transcend the moment and perceive the larger in which that moment was occurring. To be able to do this is to lift above such labels as good and evil and to be present only to what is. When we are in such alignment, without feeling or judgment, we see what is true, what is real. To receive everything and everyone as beautiful is to see as the God-force itself "sees."

After a visit to the United States National Holocaust Museum in Washington, D.C., I was inspired to rededicate myself to the cause of speaking out for the rights of all human beings. The example of Hitler and his murder machine reminded me to protest whenever and wherever I hear racist remarks or derogatory stereotyping.

I am ever mindful of the words of Pastor Martin Niemoller: "In Germany they first came for the communists and I didn't speak up because I wasn't a communist. Then they came for the Jews, and I didn't speak up because I wasn't a Jew. Then they came for the trade unionists, and I didn't speak up because I wasn't a trade unionist. Then they came for the Catholics, and I didn't speak up because I was a Protestant. Then they came for me — and by that time no one was left to speak up."

The holocaust began with making people scapegoats for Germany's economic ills. The economy was in terrible straits and someone needed to carry the blame. The Jews were convenient. People believed the lies they were told because they wanted to believe them. They wanted to have some group to blame. Then, if their government could do away with the group, the problems that plagued their society would disappear.

Scapegoating took place in 1990's in the United States.

In California, there was talk of how aliens were taking jobs away from white Americans who, ironically, did not want the menial jobs the aliens took. The economy of California was faltering, and aliens became easy scapegoats for mismanagement or for changing times.

In Iowa in the 1990's there was resentment of Hispanics who were moving in to take unwanted jobs in meatpacking plants because they were helping large numbers of relatives to relocate in the same communities. The locals tended to forget that their ancestors, who came from Scandinavia and Germany, did the very same thing. When their groups did it, it was wonderful, but the Hispanics were viewed as invaders.

I speak up for aliens, for Hispanics, and for every "they" I hear being put down. I may not be successful in changing the racism or the discrimination, but at least I will not have participated in the creation of those realities by remaining silent. I am **being the change I want to see happen** and **receiving these people as beautiful just as they are**. That is easy for me. What is difficult for me is to **receive as beautiful exactly as they are** those who demand that Hispanics speak English in order to be real Americans, those who blame illegal aliens for our economic woes, those who look down upon others by using labels and calling them names, those who are "racist."

For me to receive them as beautiful, I must breathe and I must remember that they are playing out their part in the whole. I am not receiving them if I resort to labeling them or calling them names, or blaming them as the real creators of our societal ills. I breathe and know that while I strongly disagree with them and will challenge their propaganda, they are no less important to the whole.

We each play a unique role in the unfolding life saga. It is limiting to label that role good or bad. We are doing what there is for us to do and very few of us have vision great enough to perceive the whole or the long-term effects of our actions.

Judas was neither good nor bad. He had a role to play. It was his task to clear the way for the fulfillment of Jesus' mission. Jesus himself is reported to have said, "One of you will betray me." He knew of his greater destiny and he knew what would contribute to his journey to that destiny.

* * *

This brings us to the remaining words in the principle **receive all people as beautiful "exactly as they are."** Even this little phrase has been a source of aggravation to many people.

How often has one of us said of another, "I'll receive her as beautiful, but not as she is. When she changes (whatever) then she will be fine. Then, I will be able to receive her as beautiful."

Again, this is not good enough if we want to embody the unconditional nature of *conscious loving*.

To **receive others exactly as they are** is to acknowledge that they are functioning in their evolving perfection. We may not understand why they are the way they are. We may not like the way they are. We may not want them to be the way they are. However, our thoughts and feelings are not the criteria for how they ought to be.

* * *

For everything there is a season. But, more than that, for everything there is a reason. Practicing the six **Love Principles** enables us to remain open to what we do not understand and to wait for further clarification. Everything that happens is part of a larger whole and is therefore to be received as beautiful exactly as it is, even when we don't yet understand it.

For example, what if the stomach cell was to develop cancer? Would it be evil? No. It would be of God because everything is of God. We call cancer a disease. We rue it because it leads to suffering and often to death. But cancer is also part of a larger perfection and part of the evolutionary process.

Radiation and chemical therapy are the key

treatments for what we call cancer. What if we human beings need to change our genetic code in order to live in an environment that is increasingly saturated with radiation and chemicals? What if cancer is a facilitator of that change? What if erratic cells are calling our attention to our need for strength to "live through" the treatment, that is to build our tolerance for radiation and chemicals?

If this were so, then those who deal with cancer, and especially those who undergo the standard treatments, would be contributing to the evolution of humanity. It will be generations before we have gathered enough data to confirm or refute this conjecture, but it is important that we remain open to all possibilities in relation to this disease as we continue to find our way toward healing.

* * *

Imperative to **receiving all people as beautiful exactly as they are** is *wanting to*. That is the very first step. Wanting to open the heart center, wanting to be unconditionally loving, sets the process in motion and prepares us for the actual doing.

If we do not want to embody this principle, we will discover that it is very easy to continue in our judgments and ill feelings. It is a habit well ingrained. We will continue to live in our chosen way, but we will not evolve as we might because we will maintain our sense of separation from the whole.

The paradox is that while we perpetuate the sense of separation, we will, in fact, not be separate because, by our very nature, we are part of the whole.

If we want to embody this principle, our next

task is to learn to breathe consciously. Breathing facilitates receiving. It helps to expand the chest, which helps to open the way for heart center energy. Breathing keeps our energy flowing.

Any time we encounter someone we don't like, or in relation to whom we create fear, one of the first things we do instinctively is to stop breathing. Whenever we do this we immobilize ourselves. We put our most useful faculties on hold just when we need them most. We sever our conscious connection with the source when we cut off our breath flow.

If we want to receive someone, we need to take a deep breath. And then take another. We will begin to feel how we are empowering ourselves as we do this. *We draw in options and release creative action.* The breath enables us to be in the flow of what is transpiring and to make choices that serve us.

Releasing is a next important step. We breathe in energy from the source and we breathe in the energy of the one in front of us. Then, we exhale. We release the dynamic. We release the energy. We do not cling to any part of the transaction or to our experience of the person. We continue to empower ourselves to make new choices.

Every time we breathe fully and consciously, we expand our own fields. In doing so, we expand past our own limited perceptions of the person and of the circumstance. We immediately open to possibilities that we did not see a second before.

This process also applies to persons we love. We do not cling to them or hold on to what we value. We release, on the breath, and open ourselves to the new and the next that is there for us to discover in relation to this other. This practice keeps the relationship alive and growing.

When **we receive others as beautiful exactly as they are**, we encourage their growth. By loving them, we affirm their ability to grow. We unconditionally welcome them in the present moment, thereby embracing their potential to become something new, something more. We foster the evolutionary process and discover how to love consciously.

* * *

Receiving all people as beautiful exactly as they are begins with receiving self. We cannot unconditionally love others if we do not unconditionally love self.

If we are unhappy with something we did, we can redo it. We do not have to berate ourselves in the process. Being hard on self leads to stress, and to an inner environment of negativity. It does not foster the creative process. We can forgive ourselves. We can love ourselves, and go on.

When I graduated from high school, my college entrance exam scores were not high enough for me to get into day classes at the University. I was devastated and too ashamed to tell anyone. I could not let anyone know that I had had reading problems throughout my school career. The problems affected me most adversely during test taking, because I would freeze up as I read the questions and be unable to think of any response. When I ruined my chance for direct admission to college, I berated myself as stupid and saw myself as unintelligent. I carried this self-imposed stigma for years. Nonetheless, I managed to earn an A.A. and B.A., attending night school. I then went on to earn an M.F.A. and I was eventually advanced to candidacy for a

Ph.D. It was then that I began to open to **receive myself as beautiful.**

I started by feeling compassion for the part of myself that had trouble reading. I later learned that I was dyslexic. I embraced myself and breathed, acknowledging my seeming limitations. I soon realized that I had concocted methods for surviving in school that reflected my intelligence. Whenever I was to take a test, I would not only study diligently, I would ask myself questions I thought the teacher would ask. Then, I would research and write essays for each of about five such questions and memorize them. Invariably, when the test was placed in front of me, two or three of the questions I had thought of and prepared for were on the test. I could simply spill out what I had committed to memory. In this manner, I made my way through school. When I looked back on this, I saw that it took savvy to predetermine the questions and intelligence to prepare the answers. This became one more reason for **receiving myself as beautiful.**

The real point of all this is, however, that I didn't need reasons to **receive myself as beautiful**. Even if I never passed a test, or if I never graduated, I was still worthy of being received just as I was, just because I was.

Each of us was born of a miracle: the uniting of sperm and egg to produce life. We are blessed with inherent worth as human beings and we are equal to all others in value. We are unique and irreplaceable in the grand scheme. When we acknowledge this, we also know that it is true of every other living being. As we respect ourselves, so we will respect others.

Receiving self is one of the initial steps in the individualizing process. The human being is the greatest masterpiece to evolve in the creative design. If we denigrate what we are, we are guilty of blasphemy. If we do not rejoice in the beauty of our beings and open our hearts in love to self, we are being utterly disrespectful of the Creator.

The most distorted form of human being is the one who walks about with head bent in self-denial. Such human expressions of the life force never look up into the glory of the light with which they are merged. Worse still, such beings cannot fulfill their destiny. They have devoted themselves to the death of the human spirit.

I remember times when I functioned that way, distorted and depressed under the weight of self-flogging. I had to make an effort to lift up out of the morass of my self-hatred. First I had to want to. Then I had to breathe and open my heart to discover the beauty of myself. I had to breathe, and allow myself to go soft, to allow my love energy to flow to myself, and to speak quiet truth to replace the lies I had told myself.

Breathing and opening, we can say to ourselves: "I am a human being. I am worthy. I am good. I am loved. I am love."

It takes considerable practice to sustain this new way of knowing self, but the process is enhanced by the moments of fulfilling joy. We can feel ourselves growing taller from the inside. We become increasingly stronger. Our reward comes when we look in the mirror and see a face radiant with love and with light. Then we know the true magnitude of love, for we see in whose image we were made.

* * *

Exercises for Practice:

1. When you discover that you are being judgmental toward another, breathe deeply several times. On each exhale, release the judgment. On each inhale, focus on opening your heart center and receiving this life expression as part of the whole. You don't have to like or agree with the individual. Breathe and receive, making room in yourself for this other. To **receive all persons as beautiful**, begin by wanting to.

2. In a public place, amidst strangers and without being observed, begin to take on the walk, body shape, facial expression, gestures, etc. of a passerby. Feel yourself merging and becoming one with this stranger. Look out at the world through his or her eyes. Feel love and compassion for yourself *as* this other and then *for* this other. Receive this stranger as a part of yourself comprising the whole of humanity.

3. To know that all is of God, practice by receiving every phone call and every knock on the door as a visit from God. See God in all people and expressions, and in every catastrophe and ecstasy.

THE LOVE PRINCIPLES
AND THE CHAKRAS

Each human being is a complex energy system with numerous components of self interacting at once. Although we sometimes identify with certain familiar ways of expressing ourselves, saying: "I am the kind of person who. . ." we are always much more than we say we are. In addition, we are always changing, and, because of the numerous components of self always available to us, we have the ability to change at will, and often.

To open this potential to our use, we must first be able to distinguish between living in the private world and living in the energy world. In the private world, we think we know what is transpiring. But what we think is happening is not necessarily what is actually happening. The thinking is based on images we hold in the private world.

For example, my mate says emphatically, "Leave me alone." In my private world I immediately link this with the image of someone who is angry and has the potential for violence. I awaken fear in response, as well as a feeling of rejection. In the energy world, the mate has stated his need in the moment and issued a command. He had no intention of frightening, rejecting or alienating.

Another private world view of his statement

"Leave me alone," might have been an image in my head of someone who really wants to be loved and cared for but does not know how to ask for what he wants. If I respond to the image in my head, I will go forward and pursue because I think I know what my mate really needs and wants. I might be very wrong.

The possible private world views are endless. All distort our view of the actual dynamic occurring. When we relate through our private worlds, we are interacting with ourselves while appearing to interact with the other.

When we move beyond the confines of the private world and enter the energy world, the real world, we are present to what is transpiring and we respond to it without invoking patterned behavior that most likely does not apply. In the case cited above, we might simply leave. Or we might say, "I will leave you alone but I'd rather be with you." Or, if we want to know, we might say, "I will honor your request, but first, why do you want to be left alone?" By these simple inquiries we move beyond the private world and toward the energy world.

It is through the various components of self, and the energy centers associated with those components, that we draw energy to ourselves. It is also through those components and energy centers that we direct energy out into the world. These energy centers are known as chakras, a Sanskrit term meaning "wheels of force."

When light passes through a prism, it refracts into seven primary color rays. The energy force that gives us life is refracted by our consciousness into seven primary energy wave bands, each with a different frequency. As color is distinguishable to the eye, so these differing chakra frequencies are distinguishable to the sensitive observer who is able to register energy, because the quality of the energy of each band is very different from the other.

For example, there is a distinct difference between the energy of the solar plexus and that of the third eye center. When people communicate with us through the solar plexus chakra, our feelings are awakened because they are sending feeling energy toward us. The energy of feeling is magnetic. It draws us in and demands a feeling response. If those same people were to address us on the same issue through the throat chakra, the seat of the objective mind, the mind might come to life. The energy of thinking has a completely different texture. It stimulates analysis, calls our attention to details and evokes our opinions. Or, third eye chakra communication might awaken our visioning or our intuition. Both of these responses are very different from awakening feelings.

The chakras are all equal in value. We are not more evolved when we function through the heart center, the seat of unconditional love, than we are when functioning through the generative chakra, the seat of creative action. We are more evolved when we function consciously through the various chakras.

Each energy center produces needed and unique expressions of the life force. All the chakras work together to produce a complete experience or expression of the self. Persons are in balance when they can consciously direct energy through all seven primary chakras at will. When this occurs, we experience the presence of a whole and powerful person. We sense integrity and we are drawn to a universal quality that makes us feel affirmed.

When balance does not exist, the distortion is easily observable even if we cannot identify exactly what is wrong. I have experienced this all too often with politicians. I remember one President of the United States in particular. He had such a congenial manner. The solar plexus energy poured forth in his smile and warmth. I felt good all over and even smiled in return, though I was in my living room and he was on the television screen. But something was off. The third eye chakra was not activated. What he was saying made no sense. He communicated with excellent delivery through the throat chakra, as any actor would, but the crown chakra was not involved and I could hear no truth being spoken. He was a powerful example of imbalance, which was reflected throughout his administration.

When there is balance, there is an unobstructed flow of energy not only in each of the chakras but also between the polarities. Each energy field is comprised of yang energy, which carries and imprints a pattern, and yin energy, which makes the pattern manifest. Each human being, each autonomous field, comes into being as a result of the constant flow of energy between the yang and yin polarities.

The Sacral Chakra:
Have No Expectations
but rather Abundant Expectancy

The yin, or feminine, pole of the human energy field, is called the sacral chakra. It corresponds to the base of the spine in the physical body, although none of the chakras are actually on or in the physical body. Another way to refer to the sacral chakra is to call it the "fertile void." This is an appropriate moniker because this energy center represents what is unknown in our lives.

Pure potential rests here, waiting to emerge, waiting to be shaped. Even when nothing seems to be happening, there is great activity in the fertile void. The waiting is a pregnant waiting. Something is always germinating and will appear in its right time.

The **Love Principle have no expectations but rather abundant expectancy** is directly related to the sacral chakra. Letting go of expectations is letting go of the private world and the past. By releasing specific images, we open ourselves to what is, and to what is emerging. We open ourselves to the pure energy of the void and we impose no limitations on what will come into being.

In 1957, when I was barely 18 years of age and well ensconced in the suffering and loneliness of youth, I arrived at a desk to sign up for an acting class. The room was illumined only by the light of encroaching dusk. It filtered in softly from the single window situated behind the intriguing woman at the desk. As I approached, I quickly lost interest in the registration process and was immediately drawn to the woman.

I had never experienced such a magnetic pull. This was especially noteworthy because I could barely see the woman's face. Her body was rounded toward the desk, her chin toward her chest, and her eyes were concealed from me. My initial impression was that she did not want to be seen or known, and that heightened my desire for contact. My intuitive sense was that something profound awaited me and that this woman knew something I had to know. None of what I felt was rational. I felt pulled to another realm, to something that I could not define. It was a sacral chakra pull.

When she did look up, my sensing was confirmed. I journeyed deep into her eyes, momentarily losing touch with objective reality. I felt a chill and my senses were incredibly heightened. The experience was one of coming home but I had no idea what that meant, until years later.

I had approached the desk with **no expectations** and no chatter in the private world. I was open, and I felt myself exposed to an elemental energy. It was as if I stood at the threshold of the source of my being. The sacral chakra had been activated and I fully cooperated with what was transpiring even though it was a complete mystery to me.

As it turned out, what was in process was my spiritual awakening. The woman at the desk was to become my spiritual mother, teacher, and mentor. My life changed as a result of that encounter. My consciousness was gradually transformed. I opened to the knowledge that I was one with all there is, and I moved into a life of service. On that day in that office I caught a glimpse of the more, and from that glimpse I entered into spiritual studies that led me to become unconditionally loving and to receive the **Love Principles**.

We empower ourselves in two profound ways by consciously activating the energy of the sacral chakra and by practicing the **Love Principle have no expectations but rather abundant expectancy**. First, we remove from ourselves the shackles of how life previously played itself out. That is, we remove predictability and repetition. Second, we immerse ourselves in the unknown and say yes with the whole of our beings to endless potential.

When we choose to live this way, we are ready for anything because in every moment we are aware that we don't know what will transpire next. We accept this and look eagerly toward what is emerging. We are on the cutting edge of our own lives as they unfold because we are committed to whatever manifests. We merge with the moment as it occurs. This is known in Eastern spiritual traditions as living in the Tao, or "way". By practicing **having no expectations** and by consciously awakening **abundant expectancy**, we make a meditation of our daily lives.

The Crown Chakra: Choice Is the Life Process

The yang, or masculine, pole of the human field is the crown chakra. It corresponds to the area just above the crown of the head. This chakra is the center of knowing. Whereas the sacral chakra is symbolized by the darkness of the unknown, the light of revelation characterizes the crown.

As we align consciously with crown chakra energies, the pattern of our life is revealed to us. We know what to pursue and what to let fall away. Here, new direction is shown to us.

We wait in trust in the darkness of the yin polarity and when the new dawns in the light of consciousness we are free to choose the unique expression we will give to it. **Choice is the life process. In each new moment of awareness, we are free to make a new choice.**

After meeting my spiritual mother in the dim light of dusk in a Manhattan office, it took twelve years before I was ready to lift what had been awakening in the sacral chakra into the light of the crown chakra. The magnetic pull I had felt when I first met her was reawakened on a journey I made across the United States. My friend had moved to California in 1961 and, although we had corresponded, I had not seen her in eight years. As my husband and I made our way west, excitement and anticipation began to rise in me.

When we reached the Canadian Rockies, the energies in my crown chakra began to stir. I felt surrounded by light. As we drove through the high mountains of Jasper, Alberta, I suddenly realized that I was observing the peaks from above them. I could see the caps, the downward expanse of the elevations, the road, our car, and the two of us inside it. I began to hear, not with my ears but with the crown chakra, the music of the spheres. I knew that there would be no turning back from this profound shift in consciousness. To this day, the music is always available to me through the crown chakra.

By the time I reached my friend, two weeks later, I was ready to meet her soul to soul. We held each other's gaze for a timeless period, and when she said, "Perhaps I was your mother in some other lifetime," I knew without question that that was true.

It was during that brief visit that the expressions of my life began to change, to take new form. My friend assumed the role of my teacher, guiding and directing me through spiritual literature and encouraging me to open to other planes of awareness and to finer frequencies.

The crown chakra had been awakened. During a stop in Big Sur on the California coast after the visit with my now teacher-friend, I looked into the heart of a flower and watched its form disappear before my eyes. In its place I saw only energy. I was drawn directly into the energy and merged with its flow. In that moment I knew that all that appeared in the objective world was, in truth, energy in motion. I experienced the flower in motion and myself in motion.

Within a few weeks, deeply engrossed in the study of spiritual wisdom, I began to travel in my sleep to classes where I received profound instruction. Within a year I was ready to embody what I had learned. When I made that choice consciously, I was able to recall what I had been taught. It was then that I received **The Love Principles** and could bring them into action.

I had experienced the opening of the crown chakra and I had made the choice to be present to the energy world, to be taught, and to embody the teachings.

There are five chakras directly related to the personality self, the pattern of self-expression that we present to the world. Each of the remaining **Love Principles** is related to one of these chakras.

The Generative Chakra:
Be the Change You Want to See Happen
Instead of Trying to Change Anyone Else

The generative chakra, which corresponds to the genitals in the physical body, is the chakra through which we express ourselves physically in the world. It is the chakra through which we are able to **be the change we want to see happen**.

It is here that we generate the new and fulfill our potential. We express congruence by aligning what we choose through our knowing in the crown chakra with what is waiting to emerge in the void.

To activate the sacral chakra energies we ask ourselves, "What is it that I want to bring into being?" We answer this question by going beyond visualization to giving life to the reality that we are choosing. We become what we see. We give physical form and expression to the frequency we are registering.

Once I had received the **Love Principles,** I knew that the change I wanted to embody was to be a force of love at the high school where I was teaching. A momentum had begun in me and the vision of the unfolding **Love Project** was clear and ready to be actualized. No doubts stood in my way. I was unhampered by limitations. It was as if I were the Wright brothers. I had created a craft that could fly, and a new era of my life had begun.

The Solar Plexus:
Problems Are Opportunities

The solar plexus chakra corresponds to the digestive organs. It represents feelings. Feelings serve to motivate creative activities. However, when we don't feel good about a situation or ourselves we cannot easily mobilize ourselves into action.

The **Love Principle problems are opportunities** is associated with this chakra. In order to know the opportunity in any difficulty, we must first be willing to register, identify, and experience the feelings that are moving as turbulent energy in the solar plexus. This powerful energy is inviting us to take a fresh look at each life moment and to open to how we might change and grow because of it.

In order to function consciously through the solar plexus, it is necessary to breathe deeply. It is on the breath that we can give life to the feelings and discover our opportunities.

Some of us are afraid of feelings. We think that by dismissing the feelings, they will go away. But unexpressed feelings remain and we become congested. What was a **problem** seeking to awaken us to an **op-**

portunity, might now become an instance of dis-ease. When we suppress feelings over time, the dis-ease can become chronic. Or, the backlog of feelings can become an emotional "bomb" waiting to implode and cause serious internal damage, or explode and create chaos in our lives and relationships.

The problems that had faced me at Thomas Jefferson High School were so enormous that everyone agreed they were insurmountable. I couldn't teach because attendance was poor, discipline was almost nonexistent, and staff morale was at an all-time low. My students lived in the most wretched of conditions, drug deaths were commonplace, and poverty had broken the spirit of even the youngest children.

The problems were so great, so oppressive, they could no longer be contained. They were poised on the edge of themselves, waiting in desperation to be turned inside out so that they could reveal the opportunities they represented.

As I allowed myself to feel my way into each of the problems, I began to see the potential that was waiting to be called forth. Our students had reading handicaps. This became an opportunity to collect and distribute books. Many of the youths had never owned a book. To be able to choose a book that they could own awakened in them a desire to read.

The students, living in an utterly hostile environment, trusted no one. I knew they had little tenderness or kindness in their lives. This translated into an opportunity to bake thousands of cookies and distribute them as gifts of love with no strings attached. The students were in such a state of disbelief following the event that they actually smiled at their classmates as they transferred to their next classes.

And so it was with one problem after another as I saw inherent opportunities and acted on them.

The deep feeling of despair that I had held in solar plexus for so long had been nudged, stirred, and eventually moved by me into creative action. The very same energy that had dragged me into daily hopelessness now served to awaken me to new possibilities and to bring joy into the lives of my students.

The Heart Chakra:
Receive All Persons As Beautiful
Exactly As They Are

The heart chakra corresponds to the heart and lungs and has to do with the circulation of life-giving energy throughout the whole body. Universal love energy flows through this center out into the world and into and through all other chakras. The appropriate **Love Principle** is **receive all people as beautiful exactly as they are.**

The more we give forth from the heart center, the more comes back to us. This happens even in the presence of strangers. Everyone and anyone can sense a heart center that is open and flowing with unconditional love. The immediate impulse is to reciprocate. It is a way of participating in the expression of universal love energy.

During the experience of **The Love Project** at Thomas Jefferson High School in Brooklyn I came to know the secret of a warrior's true strength. It is to function from the heart center and therefore to disarm every adversary. Teachers who were snide about our efforts were both confused and won over by our responses to them. We embraced them and their dismissive attitudes. We invited them to voice their objections and we received their sarcasm and disdain. Having no target for their venom, they shook their heads and eventually began to wonder what it was that we were actually doing. When they turned that corner, they were ready to acknowledge the value of **The Love Project**.

The same transformation occurred with students. They had previously trusted no one and no thing. They had no frame of reference for being loved unconditionally. Repeatedly when students participated, they were alert to "the catch." Repeatedly, there was none. The most profound learning came when, after several experiences, many of the students allowed themselves to be eager about an experience that was coming. Their eagerness was met with a full measure of heart center love. They were not only not disappointed, they were affirmed in their trust that what we were doing was motivated by a genuine desire to bring happiness.

The Throat Chakra: Provide Others with Opportunities To Give

The throat chakra, corresponding to the ears, mouth, throat and vocal cords, enables us to name the differing manifestations of the life force as we experience them. This naming in turn allows us to communicate with others, to give to them and to receive from them. It is here that we activate the **Love Principle provide others with the opportunity to give**.

In the years prior to my awakening in consciousness, I used this chakra primarily as a means of communicating. I also misused it as a center of control. I constantly told others how things should be. I made demands. I sought to structure events to meet my pre-determined outcomes. I rarely asked anyone for anything and preferred to do everything myself.

When I was stricken with heart disease in 1968, much of the controlling behavior fell away. I was at the mercy of life even as I clung to it. My subsequent spiritual studies took me beyond self-focus and to an awareness of my place in a grand mosaic. By the time I was embodying the **Love Principles** during **The Love Project**, I had added asking to my penchant for telling. It was during **The Love Project** that I first learned about **providing others with the opportunity to give.**

We needed supplies, talent, cooperation, extra hands, skills, and equipment to carry out our various projects. Every one of these needs was an opportunity to ask. In addition, we needed top-level permission to create radical realities. There was no end to what needed to be requested. I **provided others with opportunities to give** again and again, on a daily basis, though until then it had been foreign behavior. Every time I asked, I discovered all over again that people like to be asked, that they want to give, that giving brings them joy, and, that they do give, sometimes even more than was asked.

Discovering this aspect of the throat chakra opened me to have greater faith in the human race.

The Third Eye Chakra: Create Your Own Reality Consciously

The third eye chakra is the chakra that, when developed, allows us to 'see' energy frequencies. Corresponding to the center of the forehead, above the eyes, it is here that we register intuitions. We 'see' what we are telling ourselves. We guide ourselves by what we observe. Then we apply the **Love Principle create your own reality consciously**, and activate choices based our ability to hold an overview of life as it is transpiring.

During the time of **The Love Project** at the high school in Brooklyn, a journalist and a photographer from *Look Magazine* were assigned to do a story on the unfolding events. I was very pleased that the power of love was going to be highlighted in a major magazine until I saw that the focus of the article was going to be on me as a heroine in the midst of hopelessness.

Through the overview perspective of the third eye, it was clear to me that this was the wrong approach. All of my spiritual studies had led me away from a focus on ego and toward devotion to serving the larger Will. We were **consciously creating a reality** of love as a powerful force that could bring positive change even in the midst of the hell of a burned-out ghetto. That was happening. Learning, relating, caring and hope were re-placing all the forms of death that existed. It was love that was accomplishing this. The love was being ex-pressed through those of us who were consciously choosing to embody it, but the focus needed to be on the love and not on any of us as personalities.

The third eye overview made it clear that if the fo-cus was on the love, then anyone who caught the vision could be an equal agent of change and would not need to depend on others for heroic acts.

The *Look Magazine* people told me that the story needed to be personality-oriented because that is what sold magazines. My intuition told me that the thrust of the project would be diminished by such a presentation and I wished that they would break through to see a larger perspective and change their approach. Alas, they did not. However, the story never ran.

Look Magazine folded two weeks before the story was scheduled. My sense was that the whole event was being held in third eye energy, and because it was not in harmony with how the whole was unfolding, it didn't have a chance of being presented in the fashion required by journalism. My intuition was confirmed.

The one thing that was accomplished was that the journalist and the photographer were personally deeply touched by what they witnessed as they followed us from activity to activity. The photographer had covered wars and other horrendous events during her significant career. I watched her hard-boiled approach soften. I watched as tears filled her eyes on numerous occasions when she was touched by actions of love and kindness.

In the overview of third eye center, the story had been covered just as fully as we had been enveloped by it.

The life force is moving powerfully through all the chakras at all times. If we are functioning consciously, and observing, and making choices, we can move powerfully through each of the chakras by riding the energy that is there.

If we are present to this transaction, we can choose to direct that energy to someone in our life or to the world at large. By doing this we become a conduit for consciousness and by our very action we contribute toward bringing a state of grace into being. As we do it for others, we do it also for ourselves.

If we are not aware of the energy, not functioning consciously or observing or making choices, it is as if we are standing with our back to a tumultuous ocean, refusing to acknowledge any of the power that is roaring.

We are all alive by virtue of the fact that we are breathing, our hearts are beating, and our brains are functioning. Yet, some of us are more alive than others because we are aware of the energy world and of the different shapes that energy takes.

When we function consciously, we are co-creators and we are able to cooperate as a grand scheme we have no way of seeing comes into being.

We are much larger than the representative personalities we wear as costumes in life's multiple arenas. We are energy beings. Instead of identifying with any one component of self, we monitor all the components that comprise the true Self. We will never limit ourselves to the philosophy: I think, therefore I am. We will know: I Am, therefore I think.

THE LOVE PRINCIPLES AND THE COMPONENTS OF SELF

Conscious knowledge of the self supports and facilitates unconditional love.

When I began to awaken to the cosmic dimension of life, I entered into a state of healthy confusion. I no longer knew who I was. I knew my name. I could identify my roles. But I began to wonder who I really was, or what I was. I would ask the question over and over again. Who am I?

For a long time I had thought I was my body. After all, I walked about in it and others recognized me whenever they saw my body enter a room. When my body hurt, I hurt. Or rather, the hurt and I were one and the same thing.

But, when I experienced hurt feelings, I also hurt. Therefore, I also thought I was my feelings. And I thought I was my thoughts because they were conjured up in my very own mind and I was the one doing the conjuring.

As long as I thought I was my body, my mind, or my feelings, I was at the mercy of whatever transpired in any one of those areas. To be at the mercy of anything is to be powerless.

Breakthroughs to knowing self come in small doses during the course of a lifetime. They aggregate and wait in consciousness until we can see the light.

For the first two-thirds of my life, I was prisoner of my feelings, and my mind served as the torturing guard. I remember the night as a counselor at summer camp when I stood at the edge of the dock fully determined to commit suicide because life was too painful to live. I had wallowed in the feelings all through the rainy afternoon, and had had too much vodka in the early evening. In my case it didn't take much. Usually, one shot made me sleepy. I had had at least three.

By late night I was completely identified with my feelings. My mind pitched in by reinforcing that people were in the world just to disappoint me, that I would never be loved in the ways I needed, and that it would be just as well to end the misery. I was very identified with these thoughts, knew they were true, knew they were me. It was nearly a deadly combination.

Then came one of those minor breakthroughs on the way to waking up. I bent over the edge and looked down into the deep, dark water and a loud inner voice shouted at me, "Hey! What are you doing? You can't swim!" The voice was so loud and demanding that I was frightened into another component of self, for which I had no name. I turned and ran toward the woods. I spent the next few hours there weeping amidst the forest night sounds.

When I headed for my bunk, having spent my emotional energy, I smiled at the absurdity of the event. I had told myself I could not swim and that had turned me from a disastrous choice. Yet, that is precisely why I had chosen that form of death: because I knew I could not swim.

I didn't really know what had transpired, except that I had somehow shifted from feelings and thoughts to a higher voice in self. This higher voice was the voice of my spiritual nature. It is in the spirit that wisdom resides and is then offered to the mind, feelings and body for their health and well being. Because the voice of my spirit kicked in by itself, as it were, I had not yet taken charge of that component or any of the others. It was rather as if I had been jolted into awakening for a moment long enough to dissuade me from what would have been an irreversible impetuous decision. This fortuitous entrance of my spiritual voice constituted a minor breakthrough.

In another instance in my life, I sought to prove to myself that I had completely overcome the heart disease that had struck in 1968. I had been able to take long walks, even up hill, without needing to stop and rest several times along the way. I could climb stairs without losing my breath. I could dance and engage in sports. What I couldn't do was run. I told this to a friend who jogged as if it was his religion, and **provided him with the opportunity to give** to me. Pete suggested that I begin running one minute a day for a week, then two minutes a day the second week, and on up from there in the same fashion.

In my body, with which I was identified at the time, I felt this suggestion would not work. My mind jumped in to confirm that I would never last and that I would probably have a heart attack in the process. I was identified with feelings of fear and discouragement.

A mini breakthrough occurred when the same voice that had boomed at me on the dock, tolled as a bell of truth inside my head and told me I would never know unless I began the practice.

In this case, determination played a large role. I didn't know to what component of self to link the determination but I did know that it was there and it was strong in me.

I began Pete's suggested regimen. I wanted to run

a total of three miles. I wanted to know that I could do it. The determination urged me on and the inner voice kept affirming that I could do it.

Thirty weeks later I was in Switzerland on a holiday. On the morning I set out on my run, I could feel my body holding back. My mind was active. It was informing me that I was in high altitude and that running there would be very dangerous. It was that suggestion that affected my body. My feelings jumped in with fear and apprehension. My mind threw in horrifying "What ifs?"

A mini breakthrough occurred when *I* stilled my mind and refused to allow its sabotage. My feelings quieted almost immediately and my body came back to full capacity. I still did not know who the "I" was who had stilled my mind. I thought it was the power of my determination.

I began my run. It was all up hill. It was a glorious, sunny morning with a nip in the air that filled my chest with cooling air. The more I continued on the incline, the more I was able. I saw a stunning mountain peak in the distance ahead of me. It was covered with green trees and had a shining dome of snow at its crown. I fixed my gaze on that distant mountain and the blue sky and the white clouds. I ran and I ran, becoming more exhilarated with each charge forward.

A major breakthrough came as I merged with the running, the scene, the breath, and the body. Suddenly I knew, it was *I* who was running. I was using my body, but it was I who was running. I knew that I could run forever. I knew that I could do anything. I was not my body. I was not my feelings. I was not my mind. I was not my spiritual nature. I was something more than any of the components combined. I was an expression of consciousness and I could do anything.

Who am I? I am the creative power, the power to be conscious. I am the one who activates the primary components of self. I select the quality of energy I express through the corresponding chakras.

Who am I? I am the designer of my life. Through my conscious choices I maintain creative jurisdiction over all components of my self. It is I who awaken my spirit. It is I who determine what feelings I will feel and I who monitor what thoughts I will allow to influence my life. It is I who create and recreate my physical form on a daily basis. It is I who draw upon the wisdom available to me and turn it into realities.

The Components of Self

I am making arbitrary delineations within the self; namely, physical, emotional, mental, and spiritual, in order to bring each more clearly into observation. In truth we are all whole beings. However, to function in wholeness it is necessary for us to maintain balance among the four components of self. To do this we need knowledge of each. We also need to develop the ability to direct our energy through each component so that what we bring into being is in harmony with our life purpose and our place in the larger whole.

As infants, our arms and legs flail about with no seeming direction. We do not even know that these arms and legs are ours. It is only with the rudimentary development of awareness that we become conscious that we can direct the course our arms will take. This is the beginning of coming to know that there is an "I" who is greater than any of the parts of self.

Childhood is a time of perfecting our reign over the

body, of discovering limits, and of pushing through those. As we move into adolescence we become more aware of our feelings and thoughts. We come to know that it also possible for us to have power over these, though most often we seem to be prisoners of them.

Knowing begins to dawn in our early twenties, the time for the onset of spiritual awareness and potential breakthroughs. The breakthroughs prepare us for coming to know ourselves as the power-to-be-consciousness, as the one who has creative jurisdiction over all the components of self.

Often, people relegate this knowing to what they call their "Higher Self." But if we say, "I have a Higher Self," who is the "I" who is speaking? The "I" is consciousness expressing itself through body, feelings, mind, and spirit.

The Physical Body

This component of self enables us to make our inner world of knowing and intuition visible and capable of being experienced with the five senses. It is through our bodies that we can **be the change we want to see happen** and make choices manifest. Our bodies allow us to reach out to others and to **provide them with opportunities to give** to us.

It would appear that we are *in* our bodies but we might ask ourselves precisely where that would be. We might say we reside in our solar plexus area because of how much time we spend with our feelings and how much of our focus is on food. In our loftier moments, we might think that we dwell inside our heads. At least if that were the case we could be at the controls, always in charge of the command post. If God lives in heaven, surely we live in our heads.

What I have come to know is that I do not live in my body at all. I live *through* my body. I am a large energy being and, therefore, *my body lives in me*. I am responsible for its shape, health, responsiveness, and flexibility, as well as its congruity of communication. When people say they have had an "out-of-the-body" experience, what they really mean is that they have shifted away from their identification of self *as body*. Instead, they touched the larger awareness in which they truly function. From that vantagepoint, they were able to see the body they once thought to be self.

Our bodies live in us. This knowledge makes the contemplation of dying much easier. When we are ready to make a transition, we simply drop what we have been holding as a configuration of units of energy, and the body, which served as our portable instrument of expression, falls away.

The body enables us to experience life as we are living it. In this way we can come to know ourselves. We sense that a parallel with the greater Creative Principle is the same: the universe represents the body of God, and the Creative Force experiences Itself and continues to grow and evolve through it.

The most direct link between consciousness and the body is breath. As breath was breathed into humankind in the beginning, so now we breathe life-giving energy into our bodies each moment. This not only sustains our life expression but also provides sustenance for our minds, feelings and spirits.

The Emotional Nature
The center of feeling energy is most directly associated with the solar plexus. This is a very active and

sensitive chakra, able to be stimulated easily and quickly. Feelings "happen" so fast that unless we are aware and present to what is transpiring in us, we can "find ourselves" having a feeling. Were we to develop creative jurisdiction over the feeling nature, we would sense the stirring of energy in the solar plexus and then make a conscious choice about the specific feeling to create. We would then not just have a feeling, we would bring one into being. This would afford us greater power not only because we would be the one to choose, but because we would consciously direct our energy into the feeling and its expression. It is through the emotional nature that we acknowledge **problems** and, with the help of the spiritual component, come to know that these **are opportunities**.

The solar plexus, being magnetic in nature, enables us to affect others emotionally. Our communication through feelings is akin to a demand that is difficult to ignore. It calls for response and interaction on the part of another. If the recipient meets our feelings with a thinking response, the difference between the two communications will be palpable. Feelings are visceral and involving, whereas thoughts are cerebral and distant.

The feeling nature and the physical body work together as if they were wedded. It is almost impossible to feel and not have that feeling be visible through the physical component. So often people will tell me they are not uptight, yet the tension in their face, their hands, their neck, speaks a different truth. A friend will say he is not distressed, yet a pall descends over his skin, or his eyes moisten. It is very difficult to mask feelings because even as an attempt is made to hide them, the attempt itself is physically visible.

Feelings are key to our functioning because they enable us to move beyond thoughts and opinions to the level of knowing. When we touch an insight or an inner truth, it is our feeling nature that validates it.

Feelings are a motivating force, providing us with the incentive to express ourselves, to perform actions, and to relate to others. So many times our minds will say, "I think I should clean my desk now." Yet, we rarely get up and follow its command. It is only when we feel like cleaning our desks that we take action.

We know that the feeling nature is present when we hear ourselves say, "I want," or "I need," or "I feel." The solar plexus speaks in feelings and is never satisfied with a "should" or "ought" response. It is always more important for the feeling nature to draw on a "what" or a "how" than a "why." What do I want to do? How shall I do it? Rather than, Why should I do it?

Sometimes the feeling nature seeks to take over in unhealthy or trouble-causing ways. We can hear ourselves saying, "I want to buy a new car and I don't care how I have to pay for it." This is a perfect opportunity to call upon other components of the self. Our minds would be quick to point up all the reasons why this would not be feasible. "If you get yourself into debt, you'll be there forever." Or, "A new car will cost you more in taxes and insurance." Or, "Then you'll need a whole new wardrobe so you can look good behind the wheel!"

Our spiritual component could easily show us the big picture of how this would not be in accord with the rest of what is transpiring in our lives at this time. "Getting into additional debt will put you under pressure and actually keep you from enjoying the new vehicle." Or, "Before purchasing a new car, a move to a larger and brighter apartment would give you greater living space and allow you to feel better about yourself in a more harmonious environment." Or, "What you really need is a meaningful relationship. A new car will make you feel good, but it will not provide the companionship you really desire."

The mental and spiritual components of self would serve as mitigating forces, encouraging us to reevaluate the want, the feeling, of the moment, which we said we would do anything to get.

Any of the components of self can help balance the others. If our feeling natures were drawn to going on an eating binge, for example, our bodies could very quickly check the impulse by causing physical upset or illness in response.

Having components of self is much like having three branches in a democracy, each of which can override the other. In this case there are four components of self, all under the direction of the consciousness.

The Objective Mind

Associated with the throat chakra, the objective mind is our database. It stores our life experiences and observations and provides us easy access to the information whenever we might need it.

In addition to storing data, the mental component of self enables us to make cogent decisions because it sorts, organizes and provides needed material upon request. It is excellent at analyzing and at restructuring to suit our needs. The mind offers helpful assistance when we are **creating our reality consciously.** For that reason, the objective mind serves to direct our lives until consciousness emerges.

The mind is logical, and though it has our previous

feeling states recorded in its information bank, the feelings are recorded as facts that are coded for future use. We cannot go to our minds to feel.

The mind functions in a linear fashion, pointing out the various pieces that belong with what is under investigation. It lays out the facts side by side, seeming to expose cause and effect. The mind categorizes and conceptualizes but is not capable of seeing the whole picture. Its specialty is delineating between significant elements and relating them to one another.

Just as we are not the body or the emotional nature, so too we are not the objective mind. If we think of our minds as computers, then we know ourselves to be the ones who operate the hardware, install the software, and supply the data for the memory. We use the mind to recall information, to analyze situations, to sort through pros and cons for decision-making, to reason in relation to proposed actions, and to make congruent presentations or express points of view. However, it cannot operate outside the boundaries of the programs and data we install or beyond the limits of its "equipment."

We can always tell when the objective mind is active because it tells us what we should do, and it has a ready backup of all the reasons why. The rationale was programmed into us early on in our lives when we learned from parents and early teachers how things were supposed to be. Patterns of response were formed and these function automatically when we are not conscious.

To break out of the patterns, it is helpful to introduce the emotional nature in the midst of potential adherence to the mind. If the mind tells us we should call someone because . . . (and it will issue a string of reasons), we need to breathe and ask ourselves if we want to make the call. If we don't feel like making it, then no amount of mental persuasion will be successful. Or if the mind overrides the feelings, the phone call will not be very satisfying on either end of the line.

When the mind speaks, it tends to make blanket statements. It might say, "It is too hot to live in Arizona in August." The statement is based on evidence gathered and therefore would appear to be true. However many people *do* live in Arizona in August; therefore the statement *as made* is not true. We can train the mind to give us data without also giving us dogmatic presentations or conclusions. We can instruct the mind to say, "The temperature in Arizona in August is hot." This leaves the body and feelings free to respond from their comfort zones.

If we do not exercise jurisdiction over the mind, it will take over whenever possible. It will berate us for tasks undone or not done properly. It will run lists for us of places we have to go, things we have to buy, and jobs we have to do. It will do spins of "what ifs?" on every subject imaginable. One of most amusing examples of this occurred when my partner and I remodeled and expanded our home in San Diego. As part of the remodeling, we had incorporated into the kitchen an enclosed porch area where our dog Buttons had slept when she was alive. One night, Diane's mind kept her awake by worrying about the fact that no place was left for Button's bed. It challenged her with the question, "Where would Buttons sleep?"

Diane could not believe her mind was raising this issue. Impatiently, she said, "Look, it's the middle of the night and I'm trying to sleep. I'm not interested in carrying on a theoretical discussion about where Buttons would sleep. Leave me alone!" She rolled over, determined to return to sleep.

Her mind would not be quieted. It is one of the features of the mind. It does not let go. It pursues every avenue until it is finally satisfied.

"But there is no place for her to sleep. You can't put her in the kitchen, because there is no way to close it off now," it complained.

The conversation Diane was having with her mind was absurd because the dog was no longer alive. However, by now, the mind had captured her curiosity and, with her mind's eye, she began surveying the house. Sure enough! She saw that there was no place for Buttons to sleep.

Diane then rolled over onto her back, into her best "thinking" position, and resigned herself to the quest of finding a place where Buttons *could* sleep in the remodeled environment. She thought of the family room or the den, but rejected those when she considered that Buttons would then jump up on the couches. She rejected the living room and the office.

Then she wondered about using the area at the back door. But now there was no way to close off that area. She even thought of the garage, but then worried that we would never be able to hear her in the night if she needed us.

Diane noticed that Button's age seemed to change to suit the case the mind was making, but it didn't matter since the conversation was completely moot. She tried to reason with her mind.

"But, Buttons is dead!" she reminded her mind. Buttons had died two years earlier. If reason were any criterion, this statement would have settled the issue. But Diane had no such luck. Her mind came right back saying, "I know, but if she *were* alive she would have nowhere to sleep."

Diane sighed deeply knowing that the exploration was hopeless because the mind would not let go. She finally stilled it by saying that if Buttons were alive we would definitely install a special gate near the back door so that she would be taken care of. It was only then that she could have peace and return to sleep.

The mind is a prime source of worry. It can worry about anything. Because it is so good at worrying, it can easily spill over onto our feelings and our bodies, awakening anxiety and tension. When this occurs, we need to be in dialogue with the mind, asking it key questions that silence it. For example, if it says we will probably fail a driver's test, we can remind it that that has not ever happened, that we are good drivers, and that if it will kindly remember all we need to know for the test, we can't possibly fail and it need not worry.

The objective mind is much like a faithful dog. When we want it to be still, we can order it to "sit." When we are in need of information it is holding, we can tell it to "go fetch." But if we ignore it, it will wander the neighborhood, chasing cats, overturning garbage cans, and creating all manner of disorder for us.

The Spiritual Nature

The spiritual component of self is most directly associated with the crown chakra which corresponds to the top of the head. Life energy flows into the whole of our being. The energy enlivens the other chakras, especially the other two centers most related to the spiritual component, the third eye and heart chakras, stimulating intuition and unconditional love. As the life force fills us, we are constantly renewed in all the components of self. This essential renewal is enhanced when we draw on the wisdom that resides in our spiritual nature.

The spiritual nature reveals its wisdom through instances of knowing. These are indisputable. They are not limited by logic or substantiated by agreement. They are confirmed by intuition and they "feel" right. They are supported by our personal experience but they go much beyond; they are a reflection of universal truth.

A knowing of mine, for example, is that I am one with all that is and with everyone that is. Whenever I experience this knowing consciously, I invariably make a profound connection of oneness with another. This changes the nature of my relational interactions. When I am "in oneness" with a colleague, there is never any competition between us. Instead, each of us is contributing to a large work that employs us both. I can rejoice in my colleague's accomplishments without wishing that I had been the one to present what he created. His presentation was on behalf of us all. I benefit from it and it enhances what I am developing.

When a friend suffers a loss and I am one with that friend, I experience the loss as well. It is not that I experience it as if it were mine because each of us reacts very differently. Rather, I experience the archetype of loss because, in the larger sense, this is what my friend is touching. I enter into that realm with her and we become one in the phenomenon known as loss.

When I read of the plight of someone who is being discriminated against and I become one with this individual, I stand inside this person's race, or religion, or sexual preference and become an advocate. I know that what is happening to this other is happening to me and to all of us, for we are all one being.

We are not our spiritual nature, just as we are not our bodies, minds, or emotional natures, but it is through our spiritual component of self that we tap the accumulated wisdom of the ages. In order to do this, we must be clear, aware, present to the moment, and open. To be open means to leave behind the limitations of the mind and our belief systems. We need also to be free of the influence of specific feelings while simultaneously inviting the emotional nature to validate the truth of what we are registering.

I have just spoken of knowing that I am one with all that is. If I allowed my mind to interfere, it would quickly call the knowing into question. It would point to a rock and remind me that a rock is a rock, and that I am a human being. We are clearly different; we certainly are not one.

Because the mind puts borders around things it is able to be linear in its reasoning. It believes in the separation because that is how it perceives things and holds memories of them. My mind would be quick to alert me to all the differences between other people and me. Some are male, some are gay, some are Christian, some are old, and some are tall. These very facts separate me from other people. So even people who are of the same species are separate from each other. Therefore, it reasons, there can be no oneness.

My body would simply present itself as evidence to the contrary. After all, it stands here while another human being stands there. There are two where the spiritual nature proclaims there is one.

As for my emotional nature, predominant feelings would likely be fear. It would tell me that we don't even like everyone. Therefore, it would be dreadful to be one with everyone.

To move beyond the limitations of these components of self, I need to focus my attention on the energy world. There, there are no lines of delineation. Instead, a powerfully moving force is eternally active in all that is. Once I merge with this, I expand beyond my thoughts, feelings and beliefs, and enter a level of functioning and awareness that easily enables me to verify the universal truth that I am one with all that is. It is through the spiritual nature that I have the ability to **receive all people as beautiful exactly as they are.**

In the spiritual nature, we exercise our will and make conscious choices. This is all the easier when we live in love, which means, allowing the life force to flow unobstructed through the heart center. When our energies are unblocked, we strengthen the will and can more easily free ourselves from limiting habit patterns. As we continue to open, we continue grow and to expand in our awareness. In this way, we prepare ourselves for insights, even for revelations. Our perspective on life and the world continues to change and broaden so that our vision extends in ever-widening circles. We are **freed from expectations and can live in abundant expectancy.**

When we are stuck in the belief that we are our bodies, it is as if we live in a tiny town of fewer than 500 people. We base everything we think on our experiences in this box we call home. We can't help but be provincial in our views.

When we live in the belief that we are our feelings, we see everything as affecting us personally and as being affected by us. We are ego-centered and it is as if we have reduced our living space to one block in the tiny town.

When we live in the belief that what we think is

true is true, we reduce our world to a single spot on the sidewalk of the single block in the tiny town. We cannot see past our own noses and our own view of what is, is myopic.

When we cultivate, enrich, and open to our spiritual nature, moving beyond all beliefs and fixed convictions and honoring our intuition, we move beyond the tiny town, beyond our country, beyond the boundaries of the planet, into the unknown. We move into the universal realm, which is larger than time and space. In that realm all things are possible.

We must be careful that when we enter the realm of spiritual awareness, we do not corrupt the purity of our registry of wisdom and insight. We can do this so easily if we are really functioning through the mind while convincing ourselves that it is spirit. We can tell when this happens, because we will be rigid rather than open, dogmatic rather than exploratory, fixed in place rather than engaged in eager investigation.

The mind pretends it knows. We fool ourselves into thinking we are creative when, in fact, we are only rehashing what was drummed into our heads. When the mind tells us we can't, the spirit shows us how we can. When the mind demands that we hold fast to a belief, the spirit takes the lid off the container and shows us how the small belief is really part of a larger, more universal truth.

In the spiritual nature, we are constantly emerging and we are empowered by our will and our willingness.

While not allowing any component of self to dominate the others, we, as the conscious power that has creative jurisdiction over the whole self, can benefit from the strengths of all the components. We can draw on them at will, silence them, direct them, and consciously relate to and through them. The more we make conscious choices, the more we evolve, and the more powerful we become as beings.

CHOICE IS
THE LIFE PROCESS

Some people seem miserable all the time and others haven't a care in the world. The primary factor is not circumstance so much as it is choice. I remember sending a very funny book to my mother. Jokingly, the author showed readers how they could make themselves miserable all the time. I roared with laughter. My mother turned page after page, shaking her head up and down in all seriousness, saying, "He's right. That's true." She did not find humor so much as a confirmation of how she lived her life.

Some people choose to complain, regret, suffer, and see everything as terrible. For example, a new tree was planted in front of my community. The residents thought it was too small, so the gardener replaced it with another. Although the replacement tree was slightly larger, it was equally scraggly and ridiculous looking. Two of the residents flew into a rage when they saw it. They expended an excess of energy in ranting and raising their blood pressures. When I saw the tree, I simply laughed. It was a very amusing sight. I could have chosen to complain and rage about it. Instead, I went with the humor of the situation.

There is choice in every life event. How shall I respond? How shall I receive this? How will I meet this? There is no one way. However, the ways I choose will determine how I live my life and even what my future life experiences will be.

I have traveled around the world and been exposed to people from every background and in every economic category. The poorest of the poor on the streets of Calcutta have light in their eyes because of the choices they have made. In contrast, I have met people who are miserable while living in mansions of splendor. They, too, have made choices.

The most emotionally crippled among us are those who blame others for their unhappiness. In truth, nobody does anything to any of us. We do it to ourselves in their name. This is especially true when we are adults. We play victim and lay all the blame on the abuser. Yet, we make the choice to be victims. Or, we make the choice to continue in that role.

We say we cannot get out of a situation because the other has threatened us, but we are the ones who create fear as a response. We are the ones who remove our alternatives.

We are constantly making choices. Most often, unfortunately, we make those choices unconsciously, based on early life programming or pure habit. When we choose in this way, we perpetuate patterned ways of living. After a while, we may wonder why our life never changes.

I consider myself to be a conscious person. It is something I value highly. I practice the **Love Principles** daily in the hope of functioning powerfully, consciously, and with love. It is my way of breaking from unhealthy patterns that cause me grief. Yet, I still find myself behaving in ways I don't remember choosing. Most times it is easy to immediately make a new choice and commence behaving in a much more desirable fashion. This shift is evidence that I am in fact functioning consciously. But then there are the other times, when I don't even notice that I am caught, that feelings have me, that I'm more like an animal in the grip of instinct. I have gone to sleep on my feet and allowed patterns to take over, to possess me, to use my life energy in expressions of self that are an insult to my capability. These are moments of grave unconsciousness.

The patterns that take over in moments of unconsciousness are long-standing and deeply ingrained. Many of them were developed in childhood as survival mechanisms. For example, when I was a child and adults began to shout at each other, I moved into a pattern of retreat in which I was able to blur the sound so that I would not be present to the specific wounds that were being inflicted.

Other patterns had their origin in relation to particular circumstances. In my teens, if someone was kind, loving and affectionate to me, my immediate patterned response was to nuzzle up emotionally and make the person into a god-like figure who could do no wrong.

The patterns we develop are influenced by our needs, by our sense of self, by the "shoulds" and "oughts" to which we have chained ourselves, and by what we have willingly taken in that was mirrored for us in our formative years.

The work on the road to powerful and conscious loving includes breaking free from all patterns and replacing them with conscious choices in each moment. Because the breaking of deeply ingrained patterns is incredibly difficult, we need to celebrate moments of triumph as major passages.

One such triumph for me was especially significant because in the midst of the experience I began to see some of the steps involved in breaking free of an old pattern.

STEP 1: Acknowledge the Pattern

First we must acknowledge, ***"The pattern is mine. I know it. I see it."***

The particular pattern I dealt with emerged whenever I felt another was taking advantage of a situation, or using others, or being devious, or maneuvering to have his or her own way without owning up to the manipulation. My response was alien to my normal directness. I would kick up negative feelings that I would not express, become angered because of my own suppression, and make biting comments to others because I was not addressing the perpetrator.

I played out the pattern repeatedly over decades of my life, but did not usually become aware that I had done it until long after the event, if then. This was clearly a **problem that was an opportunity** for tremendous growth.

STEP 2: Name the Pattern

Giving the pattern a name of its own helps us to identify it more quickly and to be able to recall it more easily when we have activated it.

I call this pattern of mine "Cowardly Righteous Indignation." Because I am choking on my own observations, I cough them up at innocent bystanders. Because I refuse to take a stand, to make myself vulnerable, to take on the perpetrator, I hit whatever is handy, like a boxer hitting lockers because he didn't show his stuff in the ring.

STEP 3: Reflect on the Pattern in Its Aftermath

Each time the behavior occurs, we need to review it, discuss it, and look to see how it began and in response to what. We must reflect on how we might have done it differently, what we might have said, and how soon.

Doing this doesn't always make me feel better. I wish I had done it sooner, during the event. I feel like kicking myself. I cannot believe how ineffectual and uselessly explosive I was. But at least the review makes me aware of the behavior that accompanies the pattern. I am teaching myself even if it is years before I put the instruction to use. I confirm that I don't like the behavior and that it is not worthy of who I am.

The review is vital because it holds the potential for determining the circumstances under which I activate the pattern. In my case this was especially important because my behavior was so contrary to my usual strong, straight- forward delivery.

Yet, even with review, I seemed unable to see the cause. It took me until Step 6 before I was able to uncover what I was hiding from myself.

STEP 4: Seek Support

We ask those close to us to tell us when they see us exhibiting the pattern and to be beside us as we process the event.

This is another piece of the work that is unpleasant. I do not like being reminded of my failure, especially when I feel terrible that I fell short in the first place. But if the friend or family member is loving as the feedback is delivered, I have an opportunity to make room for my shortcoming. In addition, another can be an additional voice in my own head that I can use to call myself to awareness even sooner than if I alone was calling to myself. I **provide others with the opportunity to give to me.**

STEP 5: Remedy the Situation Immediately After It Occurs

Right after exhibiting the patterned behavior, if we have become aware of it soon after, we can alter the pattern by taking a deep breath and saying what there is to say to those who have been affected by the behavior.

This always takes courage for me because I have already behaved in a manner that is unacceptable to me. I have to journey all the way through my dismay and then go the extra yards as I screw up my courage to confront. I am exposed as I shift my position, and therefore I feel exceedingly vulnerable.

While I have done this many times in my life, sometimes with circumstance-changing results and sometimes without, my quick recovery did not change the pattern itself. However, it did prepare me to change the pattern when I was ready to **create a new reality consciously.**

STEP 6: Want to Change the Pattern

We must truly desire to bring other behavior into being.

During the preceding five steps, my focus was on not liking the pattern and wanting it to go away. I kept wishing I would not do it. I hated it and I was not **receiving myself as beautiful exactly as I was** in doing it.

Finally I got to Step 6. I wanted to change the pattern. I wanted to do something about it. I wanted to set something different in motion. I no longer got satisfaction from the behavior. I wanted to become more of who I am. I wanted to bring directness into every area of my life, even when I feel threatened.

It is wanting to change that sets the changing in motion. I was ready to **be the change I wanted to see happen.**

Making the choice to want to change the pattern does not mean it is going to happen soon. It means only that now we truly want to change. The pattern will continue to come up repeatedly and in our focus on wanting to change we need to **receive ourselves as beautiful exactly as we are** and forgive ourselves our slipping. While we can have **abundant expectancy** that the next time we will succeed, it is imperative that we **do not have expectations** of ourselves. In that way we are loving toward ourselves, which empowers us and encourages us to grow.

I suspect that I have been doing the pattern of "Cowardly Righteous Indignation" all my life. I came to the point of wanting to change the pattern because the explosions were becoming less and less harmonious with the way I was living the rest of my life. As I was aligning with finer frequencies, my former behaviors became more jarring even to me.

I wanted so much to change the pattern that I caught a glimpse of the root of the dynamic. It had to do with potential loss. If in the midst of the initial dynamic I had spoken directly to the one whose behavior I objected to and, by so doing, exposed him or her, I might have forever lost the relationship and the benefits that came to me as a result of it. Instead, it was easier to snipe at those on the periphery. The risk was too great to speak directly.

STEP 7: Breaking the Pattern in the Midst of Its Occurrence

When we catch ourselves mid-sentence: hearing, seeing, feeling ourselves caught in the pattern's web, then we can break free of our own entrapment.

I caught myself flailing in a solar plexus eruption. I was sniping, not at the one whose behavior provoked my anger, but at a colleague who knew the situation only too well. Each biting phrase I uttered was a whack at the one who wasn't there. I was shadow boxing so hard I nearly knocked myself over.

Then I woke up! I looked into the face of my verbal victim and was glad to see that he was protecting himself by not taking personally my barrage. He certainly was not someone I wanted to hurt. But neither was the one at whom I was angry. I had wanted to speak truth a long time before, and because I hadn't done it, my outpouring took the form of an attack instead.

Having caught myself in the midst of the pattern, I took a breath, apologized, reported on my own observations of my inadequate behavior, and made new choices about what there was for me to say and how I was to say it.

Something more than the making of new choices and new behavior happened for me in that dynamic. I watched the pattern explode all around me as if I had been encased in a bomb that was always waiting to go off. It splattered into such tiny particles that it evaporated from my view. It was so dramatic that I knew a life-long pattern had been exorcised from my energy field. The moment it happened it was as if a window opened through which I could see the world afresh.

Since that incident took place, I do not recall a return of the pattern or its behavior.

STEP 8: Maintain Constant Vigilance

As life presents itself in situations and encounters, we must be conscious of how we want to respond and we must make creative choices that enable us to continue to grow.

A number of times I have been in relational interactions in which I might have activated the old pattern. In each of those exchanges I have stopped before responding and spent precious seconds with myself in private evaluative discussion. I have made choices that have enabled me to speak truth with serenity and strength. I am no longer a prisoner of my former limitations.

Patterns are hurdles waiting to be jumped and none of us can ever know what is on the other side of them until we are willing to leap into new behavior as an act of faith. I'm so glad I did. I leapt from a smoldering fire into freedom of choice and knowledge of new power.

When we make choices consciously, we bring about change in our lives, as well as growth and transformation.

To begin with, we need to look at our larger purpose for being. We aren't just here, having been airdropped by a stork. We have, or can have, a life purpose. Everything we do can be aligned with that life purpose. In addition, we can be cognizant each day of our objectives for that day as a way of fulfilling our life purpose.

Objectives are not goals. They are not tasks we

need to complete. Objectives are specific inner growth steps that we want to address during the day. They represent the **reality we want to create consciously, the change we want to see happen, and become.**

Our objectives are related to our values, and these, too, can be in our consciousness throughout the day.

When this framework is in place, we are ready to make very conscious choices in each of our life moments. We are aligned with our life purpose. We are clear about how we want to function and about what we want to bring into being. Our actions are in harmony with what we hold dear and with our guiding principles. The choices we make in this context move us forward in our personal evolution.

If, for example, my life purpose is to make a positive difference in the world, my objectives for the day might be to intervene with love in the midst of conflict and to relate to others with understanding and kindness. I would be embodying my values of love and harmony. All of my choices would be greatly affected by the focus I was holding through my purpose and objective. Throughout the day, I would be looking for opportunities to practice. When driving to work, if I was caught in a traffic jam, I would consciously choose to breathe deeply and wait patiently. My objectives would lead me to this choice. Others around me who were functioning less consciously would be complaining and becoming upset. In addition, they would blame the traffic for their response. They would not be aware that they could make other choices of response.

Making appropriate choices is important because whatever we choose today affects the course of all our tomorrows.

When I was a child I heard the lyrics, "look for the silver lining whenever a cloud appears in the sky." They stuck in my mind. They resonated with the value I placed on optimism even as a young child. No matter what has gone wrong in my life, I have always looked for the sun that was shining on the other side of the despair. I never gave up. And to this day, I never give up. When something falls through, I lift myself to the next possibility. I made that choice when I was a child and it has truly affected the course of my life. So much is this so that I now continue to choose it consciously.

If persons are dissatisfied with how the course of their life is unfolding, they have only to check on the choices they have made. Those choices are determining their responses and are also responsible for what they draw to themselves.

The very good news about choices is that **in every new moment of awareness, we are free to make a new choice**. We can let go of what is unhealthy or limiting. We can reach for the more. We can change. As we choose, as we change, so too will our life change.

* * *

I hope that you will choose to love consciously and unconditionally. If you do, the quality of your existence will improve profoundly.

The **Love Principles** can help to lift you to a finer frequency of functioning.

If you **have no expectations, but rather abundant expectancy**, you will never again be disappointed and you will be eager to discover what is about to transpire.

If you know that **problems are opportunities**, fear, irritation, uncertainty, and the like, will fall away. Instead, you will be on the alert to discover your next steps and your learning.

If you **create your own reality consciously**, you will be infused with the wonder of your ability to make a difference in your own life.

If you are willing to **be the change you want to see happen**, you will never need to wait for someone else to do something. You can **provide others with opportunities to give** and benefit from their support and ingenuity.

And, if you can master **receiving all people as beautiful exactly as they are**, then you will taste what it is like to love as God loves.

If you choose to embody the **Love Principles**, to keep your heart center energy flowing in the midst of an unpredictable world, you will find the ultimate balance within the chambers of your own being. You will emerge as a bearer of light, and by your actions, be a beacon for those who have yet to awaken.

* * *

For more information about **The Love Principles**, including books elucidating the application of **The Love Principles** in daily life, and cards and posters presenting **The Love Principles**, contact:

Teleos Institute
7119 E. Shea Blvd., Suite 109 PMB 418,
Scottsdale, AZ 85254-6107
480-948-1800
E-mail: teleosinst@aol.com
Website: www.consciousnesswork.com